GOD OF THE DETAILS

The Scientific Cover-Up of Intelligent Design

Christian Bandea

CONTENTS

Chapter 1

Introduction

A SELF-DESCRIBING UNIVERSE

We now have more wealth, social stability, communication channels, and creative opportunities than in any other period in history, and yet our lives never made *less* sense. Seen through the lens of scientific atheism[i], humanity's amazing progress over the last couple of centuries had a tragic course. The power of reason and the scientific methods of understanding the world seem to have won against religions, which have deceived and enslaved us for millennia. Free from the obscurantist meshes of religious faith and confident in the prospect of infinite scientific and technological progress, we have victoriously ended up in an alienating world, devoid of any purpose and meaning. The current scientific consensus is that our universe is entirely accidental. Life was formed by chance from inanimate matter in a primordial soup, and the human mind is nothing more than processed electrical signals in the brain.

We share with other conscious beings, just as confused as we are, a world supposedly governed by arbitrary rules. There

---

[i] I will use the terms "scientific atheism" and "scientism" interchangeably throughout the book. They refer to the attempt to extend scientific practices to areas outside their reach, such as the meaning of life and the ultimate reality of the universe, which inevitably leads to speculations. The definition includes an excessive belief in the power of scientific knowledge and the denial of God based on *insufficient evidence*.

is no final purpose, and everyone is struggling to construct do-it-yourself illusory meanings for their lives in the attempt to forget the inescapable encounter with death. Avoiding the thought that we will die one day is becoming easier and easier. Over the last century, medical and social achievements have almost provided us fixed-term immortality. We know that death is inevitable[i], but for most of us, it is far away in the future, so there is no need to worry about it for now. Moreover, we know exactly what to expect: the cancellation of the self in eternal darkness. For science, death is as meaningless as life.

It should be obvious for every rational person that all sacred texts, still venerated by billions of believers, are entirely manifestations of the human imagination. They reflect our cognitive flaws, limits, and biases. They provide a modest understanding of the universe and are simply too provincial to have been dictated, inspired, or written by the Creator of the world. Failing to see this simple truth means to massively underestimate a potential text truly written by a divinity who wanted to reveal its presence. Such a text could always remain relevant and meaningful, no matter how much time passes between publication and the act of reading. Any reader would immediately and inevitably convert. Because they're nothing more than human fabrications, today's sacred texts will inevitably end up on the same library shelf as the Egyptian Book of the Dead and Greek Mythology. It might take centuries or millennia, but it is bound to happen. It is just a matter of time.

---

[i] The proponents of the singularity theory believe that humans will manage to create an artificial intelligence so advanced that it will find a way to make us immortal. Given our current technological capabilities, it's nothing more than wishful thinking.

Introduction

As religions are losing their relevance, slowly but surely, science is extending its claims of competence, more and more vehemently, to areas traditionally covered by theology and philosophy, ranging from free will to the origin of the universe. "The presence or absence of a creative super-intelligence is unequivocally a scientific question," proclaims Richard Dawkins, one of the most famous and dedicated apostles of scientific atheism. The tyranny of religions is gradually replaced by the absolutism of science. We're being asked to outsource our most fundamental intuitions and our curiosity for the mysteries of life and the universe. Some agree, without realizing that science is, in fact, ill-equipped to answer humanity's great questions: what is the origin of the universe? Is there such a thing as a soul? What happens to us after we die?

To summarize, religions are man-made, and science can't possibly replace them. Therefore, God seems to be more inaccessible than ever. And yet, just because the intelligent Designer didn't reveal his[i] presence and purpose through sacred texts and divine epiphanies doesn't mean that he doesn't exist. Throughout this book, I will try my best to point out that he has chosen to let himself known in very subtle and elegant ways instead.

I will employ an analogy with the user manuals for mobile phones that were common before Apple launched its first smartphone[ii]. In line with future iterations, the first iPhone had a user interface so simple and intuitive that the available functionality could be derived just by interacting with the

---

[i] My decision to use the traditional masculine pronoun when referring to God has been dictated entirely by historical reasons. It should be obvious to anyone that the concept of gender shouldn't be used in a divine context.
[ii] A trivial comparison, I admit, but I hope a forgivable one given the limits of human reason.

device. A user manual is needed only when there is a discrepancy between the users' expectations and the implementation provided by the system's designer. Just as the iPhone's intuitive interface put an end to instruction manuals for gadgets, bringing Steve Jobs a semi-divine status in the process, the auto-revelating, self-describing world we inhabit doesn't need religious user manuals to reveal its Creator. For sophisticated revelations, implicit is better than explicit. If we observe it closely enough, the universe is filled with built-in clues that point to God's existence. As scientific and technological progress is being made, new evidence is revealed to us. One of the clues is the degree to which the universe is fine-tuned for the presence of life. This is known as the anthropic principle: the laws of nature seem to have been explicitly designed to allow life to emerge at some point. "The more I examine the universe and study the details of its architecture, the more evidence I find that the universe in some sense knew we were coming," observed Freeman Dyson. There is currently enough evidence to show that God not only knew we were coming but also constantly reminds us of his presence through clues that have been customized for each stage of our development as a species.

THE (UN)MAKING OF AN ATHEIST

Reaching the point where I thought I was an atheist was a straightforward process. My parents weren't religious, and I did not turn out to be either. From an early age, I figured out that religions are man-made narratives, often used as instruments for manipulating the masses. If you have any doubts about it, this book is probably not for you. There are better ones out there, focused almost entirely on distilling the fundamental facts on which religions are built until no trace of divinity is left to be found. What was also obvious to me is that humans are not made in God's image. If you don't find the differences between yourself and a chimp eerily disturbing, you're either intellectually dishonest or not paying enough attention. Therefore, I believed in the theory of evolution through natural selection as soon as I became familiar with it.

I did not feel that I needed God to make sense of the world. Of course, I often thought that it might be possible that *the world was created*, but I never gave it too much thought since I believed it was pointless. If there is a Creator, he chose not to reveal his presence, and he didn't attempt or permit any form of dialogue, I thought. I was a firm believer in science's power to explain everything in material terms. As a layman, my convictions were strongly shaped by books in which scientific progress is presented to a non-specialist audience. As a teenager, I had read about the godless cosmos in Stephen Hawking's *Brief History of Time* and about human life as a product of a long series of accidents in Richard Dawkins's *The Blind Watchmaker*. These books influenced me for years to come. There was no room for a soul in my scientifically shaped view of the world; therefore, I believed that death would be the end of it all, an eternal slumber in numbing darkness.

Later on, I've closely followed the so-called "new atheism" movement, and there was no doubt in my mind that authors such as Sam Harris, Richard Dawkins, Christopher Hitchens, and Daniel Dennett did the right thing by depicting religions as nothing more than ridiculous, obsolete superstitions. As the years went by, I did not feel the logical and spiritual debt that was accumulating inside me. When it suddenly emerged one day, I was completely caught off-guard. My unexpected "epiphany" did not have anything divine in it. Instead, it was the abrupt realization that my beliefs regarding the nature of the world had wild assumptions and speculations at their core. I was left with a world view consisting of scattered dots that I thought I had connected a long time ago. We know that the world appeared 13.8 billion years ago with a Big Bang, from what we have reasons to believe it can be described as *nothing*. Fast forward a couple of billion years, on a random planet in an inconspicuous corner of the Milky Way galaxy, a series of chemical *accidents* caused the first life form to arise from non-living matter. *Random* biological mutations which enhance the survivability and replicability of organisms allowed all the species on our planet, including humans, to evolve from this initial primitive life form. Our brains are nothing more than computing machines evolved to perform specific functions, and our thoughts and emotions are mere byproducts of these calculations.

The scientifically-backed theories about the origin of life and the universe stopped making any sense to me. They require a leap of *faith* at least as big as any religious person has ever had to take. And yet, these *universe-from-nothing, accidental-life-from-non-living, randomly-generated-evolution, consciousness-as-byproduct* theories are all considered more intellectually acceptable than the idea of a Creator of the universe. With this change of perspective, it was as if the sonnet the hypothetical monkey seemingly wrote in eons of typing suddenly turned into undecipherable gibberish right before my very eyes. If all these simplified mainstream scientific explanations sound improbable to you as well, wait until we get to the details... In fact, my sudden revelation was *a loss of faith*: the faith in a very long series of accidents that made our presence here on Earth possible.

Introduction

If you're among the readers who have already been put off by the mere mention of God (despite the book's title!), surely some clarifications are needed. I'm not referring to any particular religious flavor of the concept of divinity or to a *subjective* God who listens to prayers and has a keen interest in the dirtiest details of our daily lives. What I mean by God is a higher order of complexity, beyond physical laws, time, and human understanding, who brought the universe into existence and made life possible. The notion of a Creator goes against the modern, scientific interpretation of the world, and the explanation is twofold. First of all, the small progress made in natural sciences[i] over the last centuries has led some to believe that *everything* can be explained *within the laws of the universe*, without the need for divine intervention. Secondly, in the ongoing battle for liberating humanity from religions, the overwhelmingly intuitive and universally obvious idea of a Creator has become collateral damage. It would seem that there is no need for God anymore.

However, in the process of liberating us from religions, science has turned into one. It's a comparison that makes little sense at first, since religious views and scientific methods appear to be complete opposites. After all, religion promotes God based on speculations backed by so-called holy books, while science is free from pre-determined truths and biases, and only goes where the evidence leads, following the well-established process of experiments based on hypotheses. At least this is what I used to believe. But on a closer look, the similarities between religion and science are striking. After all, isn't preaching God's presence or absence

---

[i] I'm not trying to downplay the importance of the scientific discoveries made so far. I'm just pointing out that we've barely crossed the threshold of utter ignorance if we consider what we now know there is still to be known.

the same, as long as the underlying claims are based on mere speculations instead of conclusive evidence? On topics that matter the most (God, the origin of life, free will), the truths that science puts forward rely on arguments from authority and not on facts. Lab coats have replaced clerical clothing. The caste which asserts its ability to mediate the truth about God for the "simple minds" of laymen is no longer made up of priests. Scientists have replaced them and are promoting a world view that hasn't been *proved* correct, but which serves their interests. In line with most religions, science demands complete subservience and stifles dissenting views. It also promotes hypocrisy and even doublethink: some are afraid to express their real opinions within the scientific community because they're worried about possible repercussions. Whoever goes against the mainstream view is exposed and even persecuted.

I'm fully aware I got to a point where I'm making the scientific community sound more like a satanic cult. A sense of proportion needs to be kept. It is undeniable that modern science has had a tremendously positive effect on society, by greatly enhancing our understanding of the world. However, the rapid pace of discoveries in some areas and the easy wins scored against religions have generated a feeling of overconfidence in science's ability to explain *everything*. Banishing God from the list of requirements for a complete understanding of life and the universe has been done in haste, as recent scientific findings show. Just as religions were able to uphold their deceptions only for so long, the fundamental truth is becoming harder and harder to suppress as new scientific advancements are being made: the universe and life are the products of *intelligent design*.

Mainstream science is stubbornly refusing to concede that a paradigm change is needed in our view of the world, even though it has reached an impasse in key research areas. Many scientists oppose the undeniable evidence which points to a created universe not on rational grounds, but based on a mix of emotions, arrogance, and aesthetic preferences. They *feel* that accepting an intelligent Creator is an act of intellectual capitulation. They see God as a step back to the age of supernatural creation myths, which they're not willing to take because it would diminish them as rational agents. Fixated on the traditional scientific model, they would rather come up with phantasmagorical theories lacking any experimental observations than considering the simple explanation of a designed world.

Following my secular epiphany, I've revisited my entire view of the world, with one single twist: accept the *possibility* that the universe was *created* and separate provable facts from scientific assumptions and speculations. Because I'm not a scientist, I need to rely mainly on literature that popularizes science to a general audience. Trying my best to avoid misinterpreting any theories and to stay clear of any biases, I've reached the following conclusion: I simply don't buy into the mainstream explanation for the creation of the universe, the origin of life, and the nature of the human mind. And I'm not the only one. More and more respectable voices, ranging from molecular biologists to philosophers, express their disbelief that our world can be described exclusively in material terms. The evidence just isn't there, and the current working theories are simply not convincing enough. The specter of intelligent design is already lurking through the established scientific edifice. It's only a question of time before everyone realizes they can no longer conceal or ignore it.

As a consumer of literature that popularizes scientific discoveries, I should be allowed to provide feedback on what

I'm being led to believe. This book is my way of doing it. I'm not pretending to be someone I'm not, so I've kept the biological, cosmological, and physical explanations to a minimum, just to be able to support my arguments. I strongly encourage you to read further on any topics that might spark your interest. I hope that reading this book will get you to reconsider your view of God by thinking for yourself instead of simply following the mainstream narratives. Some might wonder if this is even an exercise worth doing. What is the use of contemplating a "ceremonial" God who stopped intervening at the moment of creation, allowing the universe to unfold itself? Is there a difference between a *created* universe and a *self-generated* one? I believe so. If our world is indeed the product of an intelligent Designer, it has an underlying purpose, which changes everything.

Chapter 2

The Science of the Superficial

INSTEAD OF A RANDOM QUOTE

I could have started each chapter of this book with quotes from famous thinkers to consolidate my arguments, as some of the atheist authors do. Ambiguous quotes from accomplished scientists seem to be the preferred ones when it comes to dismissing God's existence, to somehow emphasize that scientific thinking is incompatible with the notion of a Creator.

There are plenty of wise aphorisms in favor of a Creator to even fill up a whole book, many of them belonging to well-known physicists, but what would be the point of including them? Instead of engaging in a battle of the quotes, I think it is more useful to clarify from the very beginning that scientists don't know anything more about God and the miracle of life than ordinary people do. Physicists partially understand the laws of the universe, but not why they work as they do. They know the Big Bang happened 13.8 billion years ago, but not what caused it. So why should their opinions on God carry more weight than anyone else's? It's like believing that physicists should know everything about tennis because they have a good understanding of friction, angles, and acceleration. The best way to experience tennis is to start playing. The best way to understand God is to accept the miracle of life. Of course, this doesn't mean that I won't use quotes to strengthen my arguments, but I couldn't miss this opportunity to make a crucial point: in matters concerning the Creator of the universe, academic backgrounds do not mean anything. Our built-in intuition on God, probably the strongest one we have, is enough. Keep this in mind when you come across the next quote meant to entice you to join the atheist camp.

FROM GOD OF THE GAPS TO GOD OF THE DETAILS

In evolutionary biology, abiogenesis is the natural process from which life arises from nonlife. It hasn't been scientifically proven, and it has never been replicated in any laboratory. And yet, it is the foundation on which Darwin's theory of evolution through natural selection stands. The theory that Charles Darwin put forward in his 1859 book *On the Origin of Species* is still used in the mainstream scientific community to account for the bewildering variety of species on our planet. Darwin's idea was simple yet extremely powerful: random genetic mutations, in combination with limited resources, lead to a process of evolution where beneficial traits can end up naturally selected for the survival and reproductive advantages they bring. We're told that this is how all species on Earth, including humans, have evolved from a single common unicellular ancestor. Evolutionism is currently referred to as Neo-Darwinism, which is a gene-centered theory of evolution put together at the beginning of the 20th century. When Darwin had published his theory, the concept of genes was unknown. But despite its unanimous acceptance in academic circles, recent discoveries over the last couple of decades, especially in the field of molecular biology, make the process of evolution through natural selection more disputed than ever.

Promoters of atheism claim that gaps in scientific knowledge are being used as proof of God's existence. As science advances relentlessly, believers are supposedly forced to retreat into narrow corners where the "light of reason" hasn't yet reached. Biology is a good example. For most of human history, life has been seen as a miracle, and people believed that living organisms must be animated by a non-physical component that is not to be found in objects. The first vitalistic doctrine was put forward by Aristotle, who believed that all living organisms are made up of matter (the physical body) and a form (the soul or *endelechia*). The body and soul were not considered two different substances, but insoluble parts of a living being. The Aristotelian view of life (also shared by Galen and Paracelsus) remained the dominant one until the 16th century.

The separation of mind (or soul) and body was introduced later on by the philosophers Bernardino Telesio and René Descartes. For Descartes, no souls other than the rational soul, unique to humans, existed[i]. Using the leading technologies of his time, the French philosopher described the animal and human bodies as systems of pumps, tubes, valves, and hydraulic fluids. What prevented Descartes from going all the way to denying the presence of the soul even in humans was our higher mental faculties such as intellect and emotions, which he couldn't fit in his mechanistic paradigm. In the Cartesian dualistic system, the brain is distinct from the immaterial mind, which contains a person's thoughts and

---

[i] Since animals didn't have souls and were mere *automata*, they couldn't feel any pain, Descartes believed. As a result, he organized public demonstrations where he vivisected conscious animals with his assistants' help. Many times, dogs were used, and their helpless yelps of pain were dismissed as nothing more than bodily reactions caused by programmed responses. The dogs didn't actually suffer, the participants were assured. Of course, we know better now.

desires. The pineal gland is the seat of the soul, and it is this tiny organ that controls the flow of information between the mind and the body. The mind-body duality proposed by Descartes was the basis of the vitalist theory that dominated the 18th century. Vitalism consisted of two main doctrines. According to the first, living organisms (including animals, which had lost their *automata* status since Descartes's times**)** were fundamentally different from non-living entities because they contained a mysterious, non-physical component (*élan vital*). The second doctrine argued that living beings were based on a different set of governing principles than inanimate objects.

As biology and medicine progressed in the 18th and 19th centuries, the view that the same principles and processes govern living organisms and the inanimate world started to gain more traction, and the notion of *élan vital* eventually died out. Following in-depth scientific observations, it became clear that the inner mechanisms of living creatures could be explained without the need for a "vital force" concept. Vitalists could not come up with any proof to support their theory. In parallel, a better understanding of how life is created was developed over the centuries. The idea that creatures could suddenly arise from non-living matter (mice from dirty rags, for example) was disproved as well.

Therefore, the history of biology summarized in light of the God of the gaps interpretation is the downgrade of life from a miraculous status to a demystified set of extremely intricate, but nonetheless ordinary physical processes. The last biological bastion where dualists have allegedly retreated is consciousness, a phenomenon which science hasn't been able to explain yet, as we're going to see in chapter five. However, the accepted scientific view is that there is absolutely no distinction between our minds and our brains and that figuring out the mystery of consciousness is only a matter of time. What Descartes did with pumps and valves is being done today with processing units and memory locations. Computing, the leading technology of our day, is used to describe our brains, defined as nothing more than an arrangement of atoms that enable higher-level processing functions. Consciousness, the theory goes, is simply an epiphenomenon caused by the interactions between these processing modules, a byproduct that arose by chance as a result of evolution through natural selection. It is predicted that more advanced scientific tools will enable researchers to chart the last biological crevice in which the notion of a soul can possibly be hiding, consciousness. Once this happens, God will have forever been banished from the field of biology, we are led to believe.

The main argument against the "God of the gaps" interpretation is that history has shown, time and again, that new layers of complexity are being revealed each time science believes it has come close to identifying *final* theories. "God of the gaps" is a crude and distorted interpretation of how our auto-revelatory, self-describing universe is unfolding. What we're really observing is a phenomenon that I have coined as the *God of the details*[i]. What superficially looks like a retreat of deism[ii] in front of the advancement of science is, in

---

[i] Why not refer to it as "God is in the details", to bring a sense of familiarity based on the Devil-based flavor? It turns out that the expression "Devil is in the details", which refers to problem-causing *minutiae* beneath the appearance of simplicity, is historically derived from "God is in the details," used to emphasize the importance of details and the value of doing things thoroughly. In my case, I'm referring to the actual Creator of the universe, and at the same time, I'm opposing the "God of the gaps" viewpoint, so the *God of the details* coinage makes more sense.

[ii] Deism, as opposed to theism, is based on the existence of a Creator who doesn't intervene directly in what's happening in the universe.

reality, a process in which the clues pointing to the existence of an intelligent designer are becoming more refined as we improve our understanding of the world. Increasingly sophisticated evidence which suggests the presence of God is revealed to us and replaces yesterday's "miracles." The history of our progress as a species shows us that we could be living in an infinitely layered onion of clues about our Creator. Each time we peel off a layer and think we've reached the fundamental core of understanding, new domains of immense complexity are being discovered. It happened in both astronomy and biology. The God of the gaps is, in fact, the God of the details.

BACK WHERE WE STARTED

Not long after humanity managed to cut through the illusion of Earth placed in the center of the universe, thanks to Nicolaus Copernicus, the invention of the telescope unveiled a hidden cosmic world that nobody had imagined up to that point. By discovering four satellites of Jupiter, Galileo Galilei not only proved Copernicus's heliocentric theory, but also revealed that the universe was bigger than it had been thought up to that point. Earth was no longer in the center, but now a whole new cosmic world was waiting to be discovered. What else was hidden in the sky beside Jupiter's satellites? As telescopes got better, new planets, such as Uranus and Neptune, were discovered, eclipses were studied in great detail and comets were captured on photographic glass plates. Despite all this amazing progress, the understanding of the universe at the beginning of the 20th century, when Albert Einstein published his groundbreaking theory of general relativity, was quite different than the modern one: back then, scientists believed in a static and eternal universe, made up of a single galaxy, our Milky Way. Around it was just boundless dark, empty space.

Einstein's revolutionary theory of space and time predicted the movement of celestial bodies with more precision than Newton's laws of motion. It also predicted that light is bent by gravitational forces, which was later proved by experimental observations. Once again, it seemed that we were close to achieving an ultimate understanding of the world. In reality, yet another layer of complexity was about to be revealed, which made us reconsider our place in the universe. In 1925, Edwin Hubble doubled the size of the universe by proving the existence of another "island universe", Andromeda, a spiral galaxy almost identical to our own. The astronomer went on to discover even more galaxies, and in the process, he came upon something even more remarkable: the fact that the universe is expanding. And since galaxies are moving away from one another, it means that there was a time when everything would have been superimposed in a single point. This became known as the Big Bang moment, when the universe came into existence. We had returned to a symbolic center, with the moment of Creation in sight, as we shall see in the next chapter.

THE UNIVERSE WITHIN

In parallel, a similar journey of piercing through new layers of knowledge and meaning happened inwardly. This time, the focus was on the essence of life. By the 18th century, the science of biology had already made great progress. Plants and animal life had been analyzed and classified in detail, and the idea of common descent had already begun to be debated (almost a hundred years before Charles Darwin published *On the Origin of Species*). It looked as if humanity almost had life figured out. But the invention of the microscope and the discovery of the cell theory of life opened up a micro-realm of complexity nobody had anticipated. It was a discovery with far-reaching effects that took decades to crystallize, as the historian of science Charles Singer has observed.

> *The infinite complexity of living things thus revealed was as philosophically disturbing as the ordered majesty of the astronomical world which Galileo had unveiled to the previous generation, though it took far longer for its implications to sink into men's minds.*[1]

With traditional microscopes, biologists were able to observe cells, but they couldn't make out their contents. They needed a more precise instrument, which came in the form of the electron microscope in the middle of the 20th century. This new invention allowed scientists to peer into the structure of the cell with unprecedented clarity, and what they discovered was a bewildering nano-world of complexity. Today, the most advanced electron microscopes can identify details half a million times smaller than a grain of sand. In the last couple of decades, it became clear that the biochemical systems that make up the molecular structures of life are astoundingly complex. So complex that some scientists doubt they could have evolved through the process of natural selection.

The biochemist Michael Behe is one of the scientists who started the *intelligent design* movement. In his book *Darwin's Black Box*, he argued that the discoveries made in the last decades in the field of biochemistry clearly indicate that the fundamental structures of life point to an "intelligent designer"[i].

> *There is an elephant in the roomful of scientists who are trying to explain the development of life. The elephant is labeled "intelligent design." To a person who does not feel obliged to restrict his search to unintelligent causes, the straightforward conclusion is that many biochemical systems were designed. They were designed not by the laws of nature, not by chance and necessity; rather, they were planned. The designer knew what the systems would look like when they were completed, then took steps to bring the systems about. Life on earth at its most fundamental level, in its most critical components, is the product of intelligent activity.*[2]

Behe's main argument for invoking the concept of intelligent design is not complexity *per se*, but a particular type of complexity, which he labeled as *irreducible complexity*. He doesn't deny common descent, the theory that all species, including humans, are derived from a common ancestor, and also agrees that evolution through natural selection can generate complex structures. However, he points out that evolution alone can't explain the cell, the fundamental unit of life, which looks designed. To support his argument, Behe uses the example of a mousetrap, which comprises several parts: platform, catch, holding bar, spring, and hammer.

---

[i] Who must be God, even though Behe refrained from stating this explicitly. We can only guess that he anticipated the backlash that followed even without him doing so. Leaving out God was probably an attempt to protect his impeccable academic credentials.

Remove either of them, and the mousetrap is no longer able to do its function. This is what Behe means by irreducible complexity. The concept doesn't apply exclusively to human-made objects and systems, but can also be found in nature. The biochemist provides many biological examples in his book, but the one that caught on the most is probably the cilium, a microscopic structure that "looks like a hair and beats like a whip." The cilium helps cells to either swim about in a liquid or to move liquids over their surfaces. The discovery of the electron microscope has shown that the cilium is an immensely complex structure with a motor design, which includes a rotor, a drive shaft and O-rings. Behe concludes that such an irreducible complex system can't result from small, gradual steps that characterize evolution through natural selection. As in the case of mousetraps, someone must have designed the cilium.

Behe's examples focus on the irreducible complexity of molecular systems; however, the idea that the world is so well put together that it must have required a Designer is not new. Probably the most famous example dates from 1802, when William Paley put forward his watchmaker analogy. Paley compared the mechanisms of nature to the inner-workings of a watch, to highlight that the manifestation of design is obvious all around us.

> In crossing a heath, suppose I pitched my foot against a stone, and were asked how the stone came to be there, I might possibly answer, that, for any thing I knew to the contrary, it had lain there for ever: nor would it perhaps be very easy to shew the absurdity of this answer. But suppose I had found a watch upon the ground, and it should be inquired how the watch happened to be in that place, I should

hardly think of the answer I had before given, that, for any thing I knew, the watch might have always been there. (...) there must have existed, at some time and at some place or other, an artificer or artificers who formed it for the purpose which we find it actually to answer; who comprehended its construction, and designed its use.[3]

THE EVOLUTION OF HOPE

The parallel between cosmology and biology is not limited to the discovery of new layers of complexity as soon as we start believing we have gotten close to finding ultimate explanations for the fundamental mechanisms of nature. Just as the principles of general relativity, which govern the motions of planets and galaxies, break down in the quantum realm of subatomic elementary particles, so does the theory of evolution through natural selection loses its usefulness in the nano-world of molecular systems which make up life as we know it. There are cosmic and biological thresholds requiring radical changes of perspective in order to be crossed. While physicists use different theories to explain the macro-world of everyday objects and subatomic phenomena, evolutionary biologists are stubbornly trying to apply Neo-Darwinism to the microscopic realm of sub-cellular systems, even though there is strong evidence that it's not fit for purpose here. The irreducible complexity found in various molecular structures can't be explained through the small steps required by natural selection through adaptation, and yet hardcore evolutionists are engaged in Procrustean efforts to fit these *obviously designed* molecular systems into the Neo-Darwinian framework. Their strategy is to cut off the parts they don't have an explanation for and limit themselves to working with oversimplified models that rely heavily on assumptions.

> *(...) while chemists try to test origin-of-life scenarios by experiment or calculation, evolutionary biologists make no attempt to test evolutionary scenarios at the molecular level by experiment or calculation. As a result, evolutionary biology is stuck in the same frame of mind that dominated origin-of-life studies in the early fifties, before most experiments had been done: imagination running wild. Biochemistry has, in fact, revealed a molecular world that stoutly resists explanation by the same theory so long applied at the level of the whole organism. Neither of Darwin's starting points - the origin of life, and the origin of vision - has been accounted for by his theory. Darwin never imagined the exquisitely profound complexity that exists even at the most basic levels of life.[4]*

To see this oversimplification approach in practice, we'll have a look at what's been deemed as one of the strongest arguments against Behe's theory of intelligent design. The evolutionary biologist Allen Orr has pointed out that an irreducibly complex system such as the cilium can be constructed gradually, based on a series of small, incremental steps.

> *Some part (A) initially does some job (and not very well, perhaps). Another part (B) later gets added because it helps A. This new part isn't essential, it merely improves things. But later on, A (or*

something else) may change in such a way that B now becomes indispensable. This process continues as further parts get folded into the system. And at the end of the day, many parts may all be required. The point is there's no guarantee that improvements will remain mere improvements.[5]

Orr's argument might be correct, but remains much too vague to actually help reconstruct how advanced molecular structures such as the cilium could have possibly evolved. Just because a process is logically or physically possible doesn't mean that it's likely or that it will end up happening. Evolutionists have a huge amount of time on their side and matching imaginations. Since they operate at timescales of billions of years, they can reduce any biological system, no matter how complex, to a long series of small beneficial improvements caused by random genetic mutations. The problem is that you can push this evolution process back in time so much. Modern science has shown that even so-called *simple* lifeforms, such as unicellular organisms, are, in fact, staggeringly elaborate. Even though the theory of evolution can explain *in principle* biological irreducible complexity, by resorting to oversimplified "Part A + Part B" arguments, without proper experiments or mathematical models to prove it we are left in the realm of speculation. Once again, the favorable use of time becomes key. Darwinists want us to believe that given more research efforts and experiments, the mystery of the origin of life will *eventually* be solved somewhere in a laboratory, but the truth is that the complexity of molecular structures is increasing as more studies are being carried out. Obstinately applying the evolutionary theory on a subcellular scale can only be done by ignoring bewildering biological details. Evolution through

23

natural selection has thus become a science of the superficial. It can only *hope* to someday prove the claims that it has been making for a century and a half.

But how much time did life actually have to appear from inanimate matter? According to the safest estimate, life on Earth appeared 3.8 billion years ago; however, other scenarios indicate "an almost instantaneous emergence of life"[6] after ocean formation. Earth formed about 4.5 billion years ago, and microfossils found in Canada have been dated to be up to 4.28 billion years old. To buy more time in which evolution could have possibly created the amazing molecular complexity that we're observing, some scientists even suggest that life arrived on Earth from outside our solar system. One of the variants of this approach is directed panspermia, which was backed, among others, by Francis Crick, co-discoverer of the structure of the DNA. According to the directed panspermia theory, life on Earth has been deliberately seeded by other civilizations. In reality, directed panspermia is nothing more than a pseudo-scientific attempt to dodge the devastating blow of not finding an explanation for how life originated on Earth from non-living matter. Pushing back in time the process of abiogenesis and placing it in a different part of the universe doesn't solve the problem of the appearance of life. It only skillfully evades it.

Meanwhile, the intelligent design movement, accused of creationism in disguise, simply points out the obvious: life was designed. The debates around intelligent design have been focused on three areas that are largely irrelevant: whether or not it is a form of creationism, should it be taught in school, and is it *proper* science? But what truly matters is whether or not intelligent design is true. And many people, including researchers focused on origin of life theories, believe it is. Since *Darwin's Black Box*, many more books have been written in support of the intelligent design theory, such as those by William Dembski, Stephen Meyer, and Douglas Axe. Most of them are associated with the Center for Science and Culture at the Discovery Institute, a Seattle-based think tank. However, the idea that molecular structures which form the basis of life are too complex to be the product of mere chance has influenced other thinkers not directly associated with the intelligent design movement. The philosopher Antony Flew asserted that there was room for a new argument to design in explaining the first emergence of living from non-living matter in his famous "conversion" from atheism to deism, which will be covered in chapter seven. Thomas Nagel is another philosopher who expressed his skepticisms towards the Neo-Darwinist explanations for the origin and evolution of life.

> (...) for a long time I have found the materialist account of how we and our fellow organisms came to exist hard to believe, including the standard version of how the evolutionary process works. The more details we learn about the chemical basis of life and the intricacy of the genetic code, the more unbelievable the standard historical account becomes.[7]

In the same article where he argued that an irreducibly complex system can be the product of chance, Allen Orr also pointed out defensively that "evolutionists are widely perceived as uncritical ideologues, devoted to suppressing all doubt about evolution." His explanation for this fact is not only involuntarily humorous, but also typifies Neo-Darwinism's unwillingness to address the root of the problem. Orr tells us that evolutionists appear as "hidebound reactionaries" in the public eye because they "spend most of their public lives defending Darwin against endlessly recycled creationist arguments." "So would physicists if the theory of gravity were dragged into court every other year," suggests the evolutionary biologist. What Orr fails to address is *why* the theory of evolution through natural selection is so widely disputed, both from inside the scientific community and from the outside. We've seen so far that biochemistry hasn't yet scientifically explained the origin of complex molecular systems. Science is nowhere near the point where it can plausibly provide an answer for how life on Earth originated. Since evolutionism still relies heavily on speculations, more than 150 years after it was initially put forward, it's no surprise that many people doubt it.

Chapter 3

Cosmic Privilege

A VERY SHORT HISTORY OF ASTRONOMY

Imagine being born in a universe spanning billions of light-years, with *our solar system at its center* and science confirming this cosmic model with irrefutable evidence. Would the inhabitants of such a universe consider their central position to be enough evidence for the existence of God? Try to formulate an answer before reading further.

For thousands of years, humans have lived with the illusion that the Sun and the Moon revolve around Earth. We don't really know anything about early *Homo sapiens*, but we know how important the motion of celestial bodies was for some prehistoric civilizations, based on the solstice-aligned monolithic sites scattered around the globe. Primitive humans had such poor understanding and control over the natural world that they've attributed supernatural powers to everything around them. For the first civilizations, such as Babylonians and Egyptians, the Sun, Moon, and stars were living beings or deities. Over the course of millennia, humanity has transitioned from magic belief to polytheism and later on to monotheism. Throughout all these stages, the belief that the world was created and the concept of a soul have remained constant. Behind these beliefs is our privileged status in the natural world, and for a long time, this included being the center of everything.

The world is designed in such a way that the geocentric model was inevitable at an early stage in the human species' journey to understand the universe. For a terrestrial observer, the Earth seems stationary, and the celestial bodies seem to revolve around it. It's no surprise that the first mechanical model of the world, conceived by the Greek philosopher Anaximander in the 6th century BC, was a geocentric one. Anaximander believed that the Earth was shaped like a cylinder and that it was placed in perfect equilibrium in the center of the universe. The Sun, the Moon, and the stars were three rings filled with fire that surrounded Earth, the Sun being the most distant and the stars the closest to us. Their visible parts (the discs) were nothing but holes in the rings, through which the fire could be seen. With few exceptions[i], all the Greek astronomical models that followed had Earth in the center of the universe and the heavenly bodies orbiting it.

Later on, the astronomical paradigm of a central Earth was passed on to the Romans. The stoic philosopher Seneca perfectly illustrated it by suggesting that the restlessness of the human spirit was caused by the perpetual motion of celestial bodies. For Seneca, the human mind wasn't made up of "heavy, earthly material," but instead came down from a "heavenly spirit".

> *(...) heavenly things are by nature always in motion,*
> *fleeing and driven on extremely fast. Look at the*
> *planets which light up the world: not one is at rest.*

---

[i] In the 5th century BC, the Pythagorean philosopher Philolaus created a model in which the Sun, the Moon, and all the planets, including Earth, rotated around a "central fire," the same fire Prometheus stole from the gods and offered to humanity. Almost two centuries later, Aristarchus hypothesized that the Earth was revolving around the Sun. None of these theories gained widespread acceptance.

The sun glides constantly, moving on from place to place, and although it revolves with the universe its motion is nevertheless opposite to that of the firmament itself: it races through all the signs of the zodiac and never stops; its motion is everlasting as it journeys from one point to another. All the planets forever move round and pass by: as the constraining law of nature has ordained they are borne from point to point. When through fixed periods of years they have completed their courses they will start again upon their former circuit. How silly then to imagine that the human mind, which is formed of the same elements as divine beings, objects to movement and change of abode, while the divine nature finds delight and even self-preservation in continual and very rapid change.[8]

The illusion of cosmic centrality consolidated humanity's innate intuition that the world was created by a supernatural power and that humans are more than just matter. It made us feel privileged and special, and also strengthened our belief that the miracle of life can't be reduced to random causes. Claudius Ptolemy didn't fundamentally change the structure of the previous cosmological models. The Almagest, the astronomical treaty that he published in the second century AD and which would remain unchallenged for more than 1400 years, depicted the universe as a sphere, with Earth at its center. What Ptolemy improved was the ability to predict the motion of the celestial bodies, and he did so by essentially using mathematical tricks, such as epicycles (imaginary small circles in which the planets were assumed to move in addition to their main orbits around Earth). Even though it did not reflect reality, the Ptolemaic model made use of creative geometry to represent the movements of the Sun, the Moon, and the planets as observed without sophisticated astronomical instruments. It was false, but it matched the heavenly motions precisely enough. The accuracy of Ptolemy's system was improved in the following centuries by adding more and more epicycles and thus complicating the model. The heliocentric theory proposed by Nicolaus Copernicus in the 16th century offered a simplified model, in accordance with the physical reality, but it proved to be less accurate than the Ptolemaic one until Johannes Kepler refined it with elliptic planetary orbits.

Going back to the question at the beginning of the chapter, we don't need to *imagine* how the belief of being positioned in the center of the universe would impact our perception of divinity. Humans have lived with this certainty for millennia, and our mystical views have been shaped accordingly.

STILL IN THE CENTER

The way our universe is built caused us to have the inevitable illusion of being in the center of the world until reaching a certain level of scientific and technological advancement. We couldn't have possibly thought otherwise, given what was initially observable. The illusion of centrality is one of the early clues used by God to indicate his presence. Of course, the belief that humans are in the physical center of the universe is now obsolete, and it's even used as an argument for why we shouldn't rely on our "naive" intuitions, but for many centuries it served an enforcing role for the idea of a Creator. However, much like the concept of an authentic religious text, a central Earth would have been too obvious. Instead, we seem to inhabit an elegant self-describing universe, in which new clues pointing to God are revealed as we gain a better understanding of the world.

Modern science has displaced Earth from the center of the solar system, but at the beginning of the 20th century, there were good reasons to revisit the possibility that we still occupy a special place in the universe. They were dismissed, however, based on a scientific bias. Following the failure of the Ptolemaic model, astronomical theories which place our planet in a special position in the universe must be avoided at all cost. The scientific proof for an expanding universe dates back to the 1920s, when Edwin Hubble discovered that the majority of galaxies are moving away from Earth[i], by studying the spectrum of the light received from remote stars. The farther a galaxy is, the faster it's moving away from us. The natural conclusion would be that we are in the center of the universe and yet this wasn't the case. Hubble's observations confirmed the theoretical model that the Russian physicist Alexander Friedmann had put forward a couple of years earlier and which is based on two assumptions. The first one is that the universe looks identical in whichever direction we look (at a scale of billions of light-years). This means that the average density of galaxies is the same no matter how far and in which direction we look. Also, astronomers can't see an edge where the universe stops, after which there is nothingness. The second assumption is that the universe looks the same if observed from any other point. In Friedmann's model, all the galaxies are moving away from each other; therefore, there is no center. Stephen Hawking used the example of a spotty balloon being inflated. As it expands, the distance between any two points increases, but at the same time, there is no center of expansion. There is no

---

[i] Some galaxies are moving towards us due to gravitational effects, which work at all scales.

evidence for this second assumption, but the problem of a privileged position had to be solved somehow, and the solution was based on a *feeling* of "modesty," as Stephen Hawking explained.

> *Now at first sight, all this evidence that the universe looks the same whichever direction we look in might seem to suggest there is something special about our place in the universe. In particular, it might seem that if we observe all other galaxies to be moving away from us, then we must be at the center of the universe. There is, however, an alternate explanation: the universe might look the same in every direction as seen from any other galaxy, too. This, as we have seen, was Friedmann's second assumption. We have no scientific evidence for, or against, this assumption. We believe it only on grounds of modesty: it would be most remarkable if the universe looked the same in every direction around us, but not around other points in the universe.[9]*

A potential clue in favor of a designed universe was dismissed because science refuses to consider the possibility that we might actually occupy a privileged position in the universe. For decades, the initial Big Bang has been explained as an expansion of space and not as an explosion of matter into space, based on the fact that we can't see an empty center that would correspond to the ground zero of the explosion. However, a study published in 2013 showed that our galaxy is located in the biggest cosmic void in the universe. This void has a diameter of about two billion years and is known as the KBC void, an acronym based on the names of the scientists who discovered it. Four years, later, another study confirmed not only the KBC void, but also that the Milky Way is in the *center* of this vast expanse of nearly empty space. An "uncomfortable" discovery, as one article which announced it described it. "It's mathematically unlikely. But even more so, being in the center of the largest void in the observable universe would put us at a very special place, and since the times when we learned that the Earth (or the sun) isn't at the center of the universe, astronomers try to avoid theories that put us at special places,"[10] admitted Peter Melchior, an astrophysicist at Princeton University.

Of course, these two examples are not meant to challenge the validity of the inflationary cosmological model[i]. They simply show that physics and cosmology are not completely free from biases. One would expect scientific theories to be exclusively based on attempts to explain the observable reality. Instead, modern astronomy seems to include certain preconceptions, such as the fact that our planet can't possibly occupy a privileged position in the universe.

It is fascinating to observe that even though we went from celestial spheres revolving around us to an expanding universe, we actually never left our position in the center of the universe. We know now that we are located in a *symbolic center*, since every place is the center of the universe. There is strong evidence that we're probably alone in the universe, as we shall see in the next section, but imagine a scenario where multiple intelligent species coexist in different galaxies, and yet only one of them occupies a central place (it would probably make a good SF book or movie). The clues offered

---

[i] This being said, it wouldn't be the first time when a cosmological model seemingly matching the observable reality would prove to be false. Think epicycles and have your grain of salt close by!

to us by the Creator, which continuously transform as we progress as a species, would apply to extraterrestrial civilizations just as well.

They would start on a random planet, thinking that the entire universe amounts to nothing more than the stars they can observe with the naked eye (I'll use humanoid aliens for this example). They would initially assume that all observable celestial bodies revolve around them, but with enough astronomical observations and mathematical calculations, they would eventually conclude that their planet is, in fact, the one that's orbiting a star. The realization that there are other galaxies will ensue, as will the notion that the universe is expanding and that *every place is the center*. Eventually, they would figure out that the universe is an infinitely layered onion of deliberate clues pointing towards a Creator. Except they won't, since there are strong reasons to believe that we're the only form of intelligent life in the universe.

BUT WHY IS THERE NOBODY?

Our privileged status in the universe is also highlighted by what is known as the Fermi paradox. Famously summarized through a question - "But where is everybody?" -, the Fermi paradox is the apparent conflict between the high statistical probability that there is intelligent life in the universe and the fact that we haven't seen any sign of it so far. The eponymous author of this so-called paradox, the Italian-American physicist Enrico Fermi, abruptly asked this question after having an informal conversation on the topic of UFOs with a couple of fellow scientists in the 1950s.

It is a *paradox* only because we're "modest" again, this time about the possibility of being the only intelligent species in the entire universe. And yet direct experience shows us that it's highly likely that we're *all alone*. There are at least 100 billion stars in our galaxy, and some of these stars have planets located in the goldilocks zone, the region around a star where the temperature is just right for liquid water to exist and life as we know it to potentially flourish. Given that some of these stars are billions of years older than Earth, if intelligent life is as common as some scientists suggest, our galaxy would have been colonized a long time ago, and yet we haven't come across any extraterrestrial civilizations, their probes, or their radio signals. One of the first scientific papers to explore the Fermi paradox was published by the astrophysicist Michael Hart. After reviewing many speculations, ranging from the infeasibility of space travel to the predisposition of advanced civilizations to destroy themselves, it concluded that the most reasonable explanation is that we're the only intelligent species in the galaxy. And if we're alone in our galaxy, we're very likely alone in the entire universe. The Fermi paradox shows that life in general, and intelligent life in particular, are not as common as some biologists would have us believe. Being the only intelligent species in the universe is a privilege that no special physical position can provide. We're the only ones who bring meaning to the cosmic game of particle billiards.

THE BIG (BANG) INCONVENIENCE

The fact that our universe popped into existence 13.8 billion years ago as a result of the Big Bang and is not infinitely old can also be considered a piece of evidence in favor of God's existence. In fact, it has been used as such since the middle of the 20th century by religious believers. In 1951, Pope Pius XII saw in it a confirmation of the story of creation in Genesis.

It would seem that present-day science, with one sweep back across the centuries, has succeeded in bearing witness to the august instant of the primordial Fiat Lux [Let there be Light], when along with matter, there burst forth from nothing a sea of light and radiation, and the elements split and churned and formed into millions of galaxies. Thus, with that concreteness which is characteristic of physical proofs, [science] has confirmed the contingency of the universe and also the well-founded deduction as to the epoch when the world came forth from the hands of the Creator. Hence, creation took place. We say: "Therefore, there is a Creator. Therefore, God exists!"[11]

Leaving any religious agenda aside, a universe that started with the Big Bang moment is a created universe, and this is an inconvenient fact for science. In opposition, a universe that always existed and which will indefinitely extend in time doesn't necessarily need a God. An eternal universe doesn't only make God unnecessary, but it even makes him incoherent, emphasizes the mathematician David Berlinski: "A cause must precede its effect, and if the universe is eternal, there was no moment in which God could have brought about the creation of the universe."[12]

The first person to propose a "Big Bang" moment of creation was the Belgian priest and physicist Georges Lemaître. At the beginning of the 20th century, he solved Albert Einstein's equations for general relativity and proved that the theory contradicted a static, eternal universe, which was the scientific view at that point. Lemaître proposed a hypothesis of the primeval atom, which stated that the universe began as an infinitesimal point. Einstein, who had resorted a decade earlier to a mathematical trick in the form of a *cosmological constant* to align his new theory of gravity with the consensus of a static universe, dismissed Lemaître's hypothesis. The primeval atom theory didn't get the scientific community's approval. However, only a couple of years later, Hubble's discovery that the universe was expanding brought back into attention the concept of the Big Bang. All one has to do is rewind the ongoing inflationary process to realize that at some point back in time, all the matter in the universe must have been condensed into a single, infinitely dense, and infinitely small location. Einstein was forced to admit his mistake and described the cosmological constant as the "biggest blunder" of his career. Sensing the supernatural implications of the Big Bang moment, some physicists expressed their disapproval for such an idea and even tried to oppose it with questionable arguments. Arthur Eddington was one of the most vocal ones.

> *Philosophically, the notion of an abrupt beginning to the present order of Nature is repugnant to me, as I think it must be to most; and even those who would welcome a proof of the intervention of a Creator will probably consider that a single winding-up at some remote epoch is not really the kind of relation between God and his world that brings satisfaction to the mind.*[13]

The British astrophysicist Frank Hoyle, who coined the term "Big Bang" in 1949, also opposed the theory of a created universe, on philosophical grounds. For Hoyle, such a moment of creation only made sense if the fundamental structures of the universe, space and time, had already been present for the universe to expand in. Therefore, he proposed that the universe was infinite and eternal, but at the same time was expanding. To account for our relatively dense universe (as opposed to an infinitely thinned-out one that would be a logical consequence of his hypothesis), Hoyle's steady-state theory argued that new matter was constantly generated through an unknown mechanism. Basically, the idea of matter created from nothing and with no cause was scientifically preferred to a universe with a starting point, just to be able to kick God out of the equation. Hoyle's theory wasn't taken seriously for long, though. It met its demise in the 1960s, after the discovery of microwave background radiation, which had been predicted to be an indirect result of the Big Bang theory. Even though the moment of the Big Bang is unanimously accepted nowadays, the scientific fight against a created universe is still ongoing. Some physicists, such as Roger Penrose, are still trying to get rid of the initial moment of creation by reinterpreting it in a new, speculative light. Penrose recently expressed an unconventional viewpoint after winning the 2020 Nobel Prize for Physics[i].

> *The Big Bang was not the beginning. There was something before the Big Bang and that something is what we will have in our future. We have a universe that expands and expands, and all mass decays away, and in this crazy theory of mine, that remote future becomes the Big Bang of another aeon. So our Big Bang began with something which was the*

---

[i] To avoid any possible confusion, the British physicist and mathematician was awarded the prize for earlier work related to black holes and the theory of relativity, not for his self-described "crazy" theory about the pre-Big Bang universe.

> *remote future of a previous aeon and there would*
> *have been similar black holes evaporating away, via*
> *Hawking evaporation, and they would produce these*
> *points in the sky, that I call Hawking Points. We*
> *are seeing them. These points are about eight times*
> *the diameter of the Moon and are slightly warmed*
> *up regions. There is pretty good evidence for at least*
> *six of these points.*[14]

Another scientific solution to the problem of a created universe is to assert that it actually arose from *nothing*. This idea is promoted, among others, by the theoretical physicist and cosmologist Lawrence Krauss. In his book *A Universe from Nothing*, Krauss pulls a gravitational trick on the concept of "nothing" and presents it in a different light, bending it to include the definition that suits him, which is actually not "nothing" at all. Krauss's main argument is based on the fact that quantum fluctuations and a small quantity of energy are present in *empty space*. Physicists have labeled this mysterious energy contained in empty space as "dark energy" because it's completely opaque to our current methods of scientific investigation and analysis. We simply don't understand anything about it. As for the quantum fluctuations, they can be defined as a "boiling brew of virtual particles that pop in and out of existence in a time so short we cannot see them directly"[15]. Therefore, Krauss's concept of "nothing" actually does include *something* and consists of phenomena that the current conceptual theories in physics cannot fathom. It also comprises laws of physics and, as a consequence, the potential for the creation of matter. Furthermore, it faces the insurmountable task of explaining how space, a fundamental component of the universe, came about from non-space.

Therefore, we can see that "a universe from nothing" is not a scientific theory, but merely a semantic construct.

Even though Krauss admits there is still a lot we don't know about how the universe works, he quickly dismisses an intelligent Designer based on "no observable evidence whatsoever." But, turning his argument on its head, one can suggest that *everything* in the universe is proof of God's existence. Let's imagine that science will progress enough to explain the fundamental principles of our world down to the tiniest details that the laws of physics allow us to know. Once everything has been reduced to nature's basic building blocks, science would still have to explain why these fundamental components and laws exist in the first place. Why there is something instead of nothing. But it won't be able to, and this, of course, would be the ultimate form of intellectual capitulation, because science can't possibly peer across the existential brink, into the realm of pure creation. This is why the idea of an eternal God is preferable to an eternal universe: accepting a higher plane of existence where fundamental physical structures such as space and time break down and lose their significance makes more sense than a causal universe filled with matter which lacks a prime cause and was supposedly self-generated. The "infinite cycle of Big Bangs" and the "universe from nothing" theories illustrate the high degree of intellectual contortionism required to dispute the idea of a created universe. When accomplished scientists make glorified guesses about the origin of the universe, there is always the risk that the general public will fail to distinguish between their legitimate achievements and their speculations. It is exactly what the evolutionary biologist Stephen Jay Gould has warned against.

Scientists have power by virtue of the respect commanded by the discipline. We may therefore be sorely tempted to misuse that power in furthering a personal prejudice or social goal - why not provide that extra oomph by extending the umbrella of science over a personal preference in ethics or politics? But we cannot, lest we lose the very respect that tempted us in the first place.[16]

It's up to every one of us to denounce the scientists' new lab coats. When the evidence is missing entirely, the naked truth becomes obvious: some of the so-called scientific theories are mere speculations, even though they're built upon sophisticated maths. There are some voices who dismiss God's importance based on his none-intervening, ceremonial role. Stepping back after triggering the initial moment of creation would seemingly make him irrelevant. Not interacting with the world (or doing it extremely rarely) would somehow diminish his work. But on a closer look, the opposite is true: the fact that God was able to create the world as we know it by minimally intervening in the unfolding of the universe is even more impressive. As we shall see in the next chapter, the universe was built so life could exist. Everything developed according to an initial plan, which had to be extremely precise from the very beginning. Building a car from scratch is difficult. You first need to build all the individual parts, then you need to assemble higher-level systems, such as the engine, and, finally, you need to piece everything together to form the intended product. Building a car with a push of a button is a lot more difficult. You need an assembly line and impeccably coordinated robots which put together fully functional cars. What would it take to achieve the next step in automation, a sophisticated factory which self-assembles using nothing but raw materials? Such a project is, of course, infinitely more challenging, and it's a good analogy for the universe. By setting in motion the right physical laws, constants, principles, and potentiality, God created a self-assembling world with bewildering layers of complexity. The divine "hands-off" approach is an indication of a perfect plan.

Chapter 4

Demoting Our Universe

The multiverse theory is to the fine-tuning of the universe as the theory of a pre-Big Bang universe is to a created world: a scientific smokescreen to hide the reality of God. The concept of a fine-tuned universe is based on the observation that life in the universe wouldn't have been possible had some fundamental constants in physics been even ever so slightly different. Moreover, there are good reasons to believe that the value of some of these constants can't possibly be the product of mere chance. The most conspicuous example is the cosmological constant, which Einstein added to his general theory of relativity to counteract the gravitational pull of celestial bodies in order to match the astronomical model of that time. In the absence of the repulsive force embodied by the cosmological constant, a static universe wouldn't have been possible. Later on, when it was discovered that the universe is expanding, the cosmological constant was discarded, and Einstein admitted his "blunder."

However, in light of more recent discoveries in the field of particle physics, it turns out that Einstein was right the first time around. Nowadays, the cosmological constant is equivalent to the energy present in empty space (or dark energy). For theoretical physicists, empty space is not really empty, but it consists instead of particles flickering into and out of existence so quickly that they can't be detected under normal circumstances. These short-lived quantum particles that fill the vacuum are called *virtual particles*, but their effect is quite real: they cause the vacuum to have a very small amount of energy, which acts as a kind of anti-gravitational force. But how much energy exactly does empty space contain? The answer provided by quantum theory equations is infinite energy, which obviously can't possibly be correct. Such a strong cosmological constant would destroy all matter in the universe. A possible solution to this conundrum would be for the negative energy of certain kinds of particles to cancel out the positive energy of other types of particles. But this would be an astonishing coincidence, that not even theoretical physicists such as Leonard Susskind can possibly believe in.

> *For a bunch of numbers, none of them particularly small, to cancel one another to such precision would be a numerical coincidence so incredibly absurd that there must be some other answer.*[17]

In an attempt to solve the problem, the Nobel laureate in Physics Steven Weinberg proposed a different kind of explanation at the end of the 20th century: that the cosmological constant might be actually anthropically determined. The Anthropic Principle states that the universe is as it is because if it had not been favorable to the appearance of life, we wouldn't have been here to observe it. It had been put forward a decade earlier by the astrophysicist Brandon Carter, at a symposium honoring Nicolaus Copernicus's 500th birthday. Carter contradicted the Copernican viewpoint that humans do not occupy a privileged position in the universe, by stating that "although our situation is not necessarily *central*, it is inevitably privileged to some extent." The Anthropic Principle was a reaction to the fact that the universe clearly appears to be fine-tuned and also to the fact that science is unable to figure out why the fundamental properties of the universe have the values that they do.

When Weinberg used the Anthropic Principle to explain a fundamental constant of the universe, many physicists were furious. They saw his explanation as a form of intellectual defeatism. Instead of attempting to find a theory that explains the values of the fundamental constants in physics, an explanation starting from the result was being provided instead. They've accused Weinberg of depression and desperation. To some, the anthropic explanation for the cosmological constant smelled of religion. What mechanism other than a Creator could adjust the laws of nature so that humans can exist? What happened over the next decades is an act of genuine intellectual contortionism. Instead of admitting the obvious fact that the universe has been specifically designed to allow the emergence of our species, scientists have bent over backward and put their faith in the highly speculative theory of the multiverse. If the fine-tuning of our universe is too precise to be the result of blind chance, then there must be other universes in which life cannot develop, they've argued. Lawrence Krauss explained how the *need* for a multiverse theory was born.

> *(...) if somehow there were many universes, and in each universe the value of the energy of empty space took a randomly chosen value based on some probability distribution among all possible energies, then only in those universes in which the value is not*

that different from what we measure would life as we know it be able to evolve.[18]

Don't worry if you don't understand Krauss's prolix explanation. What he's basically saying is that more universes had to be *invented* to disprove God. This is how the notion of a multiverse came into existence. Many cosmologists and physicists now believe that our universe is a tiny pocket in an enormous multiverse (also known as a megaverse; the terms can be used interchangeably). As the theoretical physicist Leonard Susskind phrased it, our laws of nature have been demoted to a tiny corner of a gigantic Landscape of mathematical possibilities. Some pockets are microscopically small and never get big. Others are big like ours but completely empty. One of the authors of the multiverse theory, Andrei Linde, describes it as a "unification of inflationary cosmology, *anthropic considerations* and particle physics"[19]. It's another way of saying that the multiverse theory has been devised to counteract the undeniable fact that our world has been crafted so that we can be here to observe it. The idea behind the multiverse theory is that an eternally inflating universe contains an infinite number of mini-universes of different sizes. In each one of these cosmic bubbles, the values of the physical constants are different. It just so happens, the theory goes, that we live in a universe where these constants are fortuitously fine-tuned to allow our existence.

The multiverse theory was mostly ignored by physicists until the realization that String Theory actually has features that support it. This new branch of physics was in part developed to provide a technical framework to account for the multitude of universes required to assert that cosmological evidence pointing to intelligent design is just an illusion. As the name suggests, String Theory proponents believe that the building blocks of reality are vibrating, one-dimensional filaments of energy. According to the theory, all elementary particles and fundamental forces of nature are made up of these vibrating strings. The mathematical model behind String Theory helped the concept of a multiverse gain traction because it predicts an astronomical number of possible universes: 10^{500}. The list of elementary particles, the dimensional properties of space and the physical constants, such as the cosmological one, vary between these universes. With such a mind-bending number of possibilities, it would seem that divine intervention is no longer needed to explain the fine-tuning of the cosmological constant. We just so happen to live in a pocket universe that permitted life to appear. We can see that after our planet, our solar system and our galaxy have lost their privileged positions, one by one, the time has come for our universe to stop being seen as special in any way. It's simply one of many, just another lucky coincidence that helped us to be here to observe it.

However, there are valid reasons to dispute this view of the universe. The fact that the sophisticated mathematical structure on which String Theory is built only works with a universe that has at least ten spatial dimensions has made some physicists doubt its ability to describe the real tridimensional world we live in. Furthermore, the multiverse and string theories not only do not predict anything that has been already observed experimentally, but they also don't predict anything that could ever be tested. They are theories that live exclusively in the realms of ideas and are completely detached from the physical world. The extra dimensions and universes meant to be out there are simply unobservable, which is a big problem. In this respect, the God hypothesis and the multiverse theory are on par: they do not meet the falsification principle. For a scientific theory to be valid, some kind of experiment is required to prove it right or wrong, according to the rules put forward by the philosopher Karl Popper in the 1930s and which have shaped modern science since. Therefore, many physicists are now asking themselves if mathematics is enough to decipher nature, without the need for experimental confirmations. Can the theory be wrong if the equations are right? The problem is that theories rely on assumptions, and sometimes these assumptions are false. According to Sabine Hossenfelder, a German physicist specialized in quantum gravity, the dream of many ancient philosophers that introspection suffices to unravel the mysteries of nature lives on among some colleagues in her field: "Mathematics is a tool to carry through deductions, but no mathematical conclusion is better than its assumptions (...) In the end, mental gymnastics, no matter how sophisticated, always come down to aesthetic or philosophical preferences in the choice of assumptions."[20] The fact that these personal biases are buried under "piles of math" shouldn't fool us, warns Hossenfelder.

THE ETERNAL MYSTERY OF THE WORLD

And yet there is an unreasonable effectiveness of mathematics in natural sciences, as the physicist Eugene Wigner famously observed. James Maxwell used calculus to predict that electricity and magnetism propagate together as a wave of invisible energy at the speed of light. Antimatter appeared in Paul Dirac's equations before being detected in cosmic rays. The birthplace of quarks was on the napkin used as a scratchpad by Murray Gell-Mann. Only later were they proved experimentally. Gravitational waves were brought forward by Einstein's mathematical calculations, decades before they actually were detected by scientific instruments. As Wigner pointed out, "the enormous usefulness of mathematics in the natural sciences is something bordering on mysterious and there is no rational explanation for it."[21] Einstein was just as puzzled, and he referred to the same thing by observing that "the eternal mystery of the world is its comprehensibility."

To understand the amazing *gift* we've been given, it needs to be emphasized that mathematics is an imaginary realm of symbols and logic, while nature is made up of concrete matter, energy and forces. The human mental space is not only able to perceive and make sense of the universe, but also to derive new facts about the world, by performing logical operations in the realm of ideas. The process goes like this: scientists start with empirical observations regarding the world around us that have been proven true through experiments and they translate them into symbols, using the language of mathematics. They next perform mental manipulations on what are now pure abstractions (the fact that they write down equations to simplify the process is irrelevant). If successful, they produce new facts about the physical universe that nobody knew before. The mind can therefore be seen as an instrument for reorganizing the world into new, discernible patterns. Cognition as the ability to classify information streams in order to produce the best reactions for reproductive fitness might be explained in evolutionary terms, but the capacity to peer into the true nature of reality is a different thing altogether, which Neo-Darwinism is inevitably going to struggle with.

Our mental capacity for complex abstractions, which translate so well into physical realities, seems to be a *gift* we've been offered. If one is to assume that the world was created and that there is a potential meaning to everything, as I'm doing in this book, a possible explanation is that God wanted us to understand the inner workings of the universe. We've been offered a mental toolkit to simplify and accelerate our scientific progress as a species. The miracle is twofold. On one hand, the principles and processes we observe by carefully studying natural phenomena are translatable into logical symbols that accurately describe reality. On the other, our minds, which are still very much a mystery, as we shall see in the next chapter, are able to perform complex operations on these abstractions, in order to generate new insights into fundamental truths.

The history of science has shown that relying on mathematics to decipher the mechanisms of the universe is indeed a valid pursuit. But are there limits to the knowledge that can be achieved by relying exclusively on logical inferences? Is perhaps String Theory the manifestation of such a limit that has already been reached? It goes without saying that as an outsider and layman, I can only speculate about the failings of the multiverse theory and the mathematical model that backs it up. However, for me, the concept of the multiverse is a form of intellectual hubris. Unlike the successful examples of Maxwell or Einstein, the efforts that led to the creation of the concept of a multiverse have diverged from the noble pursuit of trying to discover the mechanisms that govern our world. Instead, they were aimed at *disproving* at all costs the fact that the universe clearly appears to have been designed. And a high mathematical price was paid indeed to get science to a point where it can say that we're only faced with the *appearance* of intelligent design.

The mathematical contortions required to prove that a vast number of other universes *exist* and are hidden from us not only brought empirical inconveniences such as the extra six or seven dimensions that need to be somehow swept under a cosmic rug, but are even pushing science to redefine the foundations which set it apart from philosophy and theology in the first place. There are voices within the scientific community who are calling for the falsification principle to be relaxed, on the basis that if a theory is sufficiently *elegant* and encompassing, it need not be tested experimentally. Some physicists are beginning to accept that theories should not be dismissed only on grounds of testability. Speaking about String Theory, Susskind thinks that "it would be the height of stupidity to dismiss a possibility just because it breaks some philosopher's dictum about falsifiability. What if it happens to be the right answer? I think the only thing to be said is that we do our best to find explanations of the regularities in the world."[22] One could argue that the God hypothesis fits just as well in his statement.

Abandoning the falsification principle has paid off in the past in another science, psychology. In the first half of the 20th century, the effort to apply experimental methods to the human mind has created a school of psychology called *behaviorism*. Disregarding everything except empirically observable events, its adepts focused exclusively on the external behaviors of the participants in their studies. Behaviorists ignored and even denied the existence of human beliefs, ideas, feelings, and desires. These fundamental aspects of consciousness were all dismissed as unfalsifiable and unscientific. In hindsight, it's obvious to everyone that behaviorism was a radical approach decoupled from reality. It brought some achievements, such as the theory of operant conditioning[i], but it was only able to go so far in explaining

---

[i] Voluntary behavior will increase or decrease if it's accompanied by rewards or punishments, respectively.

the human mind. As we all know, emotions and feelings *are* real. Moreover, recent discoveries made in the last couple of decades indicate that they are key ingredients for interpreting consciousness, as we shall see in the following chapter. Perhaps accepting the obvious by suspending the falsifiability requirements could pay off in other sciences, such as biology, physics, and astronomy. Learning from past mistakes could prove to be useful, if anyone would be willing to do it. Maybe taking into account the intelligent design hypothesis could end up providing scientific breakthroughs, just as admitting that feelings are actually real did in psychology.

Going back to the extra dimensions required by String Theory, it is important to notice that just like the "universe from *nothing*" viewpoint, the term "existence" has been semantically mutated to mean something else than we're used to, as Susskind explains.

> *What physicists (especially of the theoretical variety) mean by the term exist is that the object in question can exist theoretically. In other words, the object exists as a solution to the equations of the theory. By that criterion perfectly cut diamonds a hundred miles in diameter exist. So do planets made of pure gold. They may or may not actually be found somewhere, but they are possible objects consistent with the Laws of Physics.*[23]

The complications brought by the multiverse theory show us that science is not free from biases, aesthetic preferences, or intellectual stubbornness. Since it is done by humans it can't possibly be perfectly objective, as the molecular biologist Douglas Axe points out.

Many of us have bought into the idea that science, though practiced by humans, has managed to rid itself of human flaws. But if we intend to question everything, perhaps we should begin by questioning whether the human testing of human ideas can be so simple, considering how complicated humans are.[24]

THE HAMMER OF SCIENCE

Richard Dawkins even goes as far as to apply natural selection principles to these assumed pocket universes that make up the multiverse. When you hold the hammer of evolutionism in your hand, everything *does* look like a nail.

Natural selection explains the miracle of life but it doesn't explain the apparent fine-tuning of the laws and constants of physics - unless you count as a version of natural selection the multiverse theory: there are billions of universes having different laws and constants; with anthropic hindsight we could only find ourselves in one of the minority of universes whose laws and constants happen to be propitious to our evolution.[25]

It is a wonderful comparison, but it's utterly wrong. Extending the theory of evolution to the cosmic bubbles that make up the multiverse doesn't, in fact, make any sense. According to the multiverse theory, the existing sub-universes don't compete with one another for resources. Moreover, the cosmic equivalent of replication does not include small, incremental changes, but huge transformations.

Take two highly speculative theories, link them with an overreaching comparison and serve them in a single sentence to make your point. If this is Dawkins's recipe for disproving the existence of God, I'll have to pass, thank you very much. To his credit, the evolutionary biologist admits that the multiverse theory attracts him not because of its ability to explain our surrounding reality, but for *aesthetic* reasons. Observing that the multiverse theory is even hated by most physicists, Dawkins is puzzled: "I can't understand why. I think it is beautiful - perhaps because my consciousness has been raised by Darwin"[26].

Many atheist scientists are making the same mistake they criticize religion for: they're trying to explain the world based on fabricated narratives, which are tailored to fit their preference against the existence of God. These narratives are no longer myths and creation stories, but mathematical equations, which are stretched and twisted to the very limits of logic to produce the desired results. God is collateral damage in the war that Dawkins and his fellow atheists are waging against religions. Since religions have the concept of divinity at their core and they are entirely man-made, the fallacious conclusion is that God must not exist. The origins of the universe thus become the prerogative of science. "The presence or absence of a creative super-intelligence is unequivocally a scientific question," proclaims Dawkins. As a result, science ends up taking religion's role as mediator between common people and God. Just as religions claim to hold the truth about God's presence based on made-up stories and traditions, modern science preaches God's absence based on speculations advertised to the general public as solid facts. Sacerdotal science can't possibly lead to anything good.

What allowed the fictitious religious stories to appear in the first place was the God intuition, the natural predisposition that each and every one of us has to believe that the world was created by a supernatural Designer. Science is trying to suppress this fundamental intuition, and it uses its own fictions to do so. Paradoxically, the evangelists of atheism who attempt to discredit God on scientific grounds, such as Dawkins, actually bring a great deal of disservice to their cause. When asked to part with their strong God intuition because half-baked theories say so, most people prefer to stick to their mystical beliefs. Despite their imperfections, religions are more appealing than scientific atheism because they're based on a fundamental truth: the world was created. In opposition, scientism comes empty-handed in the war against common sense, as it faces the insurmountable task of getting rid of the God intuition.

The word intuition will undoubtedly raise red flags in any person who has a rational approach to understanding the world. After all, it was our intuitions that made us believe the world is flat and that the Sun revolves around the Earth. Explanations based on rules of thumb derived from past experience are bound to go wrong at some point, and history shows us they actually did plenty of times. But perceiving the hardly discernible curvature of the Earth as flat and failing to detect any motion while our planet is racing through space, to use the two most commonly used examples against the use of intuition, are both sensory mistakes. Taken at face value, our senses tell us that we live on a flat surface, with the Sun continuously spinning around us. Our senses are indeed error-prone, and we can rely on them only to a certain degree. However, the God intuition is not based on sensory inputs, but instead on the principle of causality: there is a relationship between cause and effect. The former always precedes the latter. Everything around us must have a primary cause. The God intuition is a fundamental one, because it's based on the core mechanisms of the universe as we understand them. Denying the beginning of the universe, by stating that the Big Bang is part of a perpetual cycle of cosmogonies and cosmic apocalypses, means going against the very basic structure of the world as we know it. It's no wonder that scientific atheism finds it hard to sell the point that there is no Creator and that the world *just exists*.

Faced with the first-cause argument, prominent atheists still resort to an infantile response and extend the principle of causality to include the concept of divinity. If God exists, who created him? It's a question that stems from unbridled arrogance and intellectual overconfidence. Encouraged by the advancements made by science in the past centuries, some supporters of scientism refuse to acknowledge that there might be areas or topics that fall outside the capacities of human understanding and inquiry. Denying the *possibility* of a higher plane of existence we can't even begin to comprehend and where causality doesn't apply is not only a failure of imagination, but also an act of ignorance, in the etymological meaning. The word ignorant is derived from the Latin *ignorantia*, which means not to know, *take no notice of, pay no attention to*. Refusing to consider the existence of God, despite the obvious evidence present all around us, just because the concept of divinity is outside our scientific capacity to study it, is an act of ignorance.

Another reason why scientists refuse to consider the God hypothesis is the alleged human propensity for comforting thoughts. For Leonard Susskind, God must be forever banished from any intellectual pursuit to understand the world, even though the theoretical physicist admits that a created universe is indeed a possibility.

Who knows? Maybe God did make the world. But scientists - real scientists - resist the temptation to explain natural phenomena, including creation itself, by divine intervention. Why? Because as scientists we understand that there is a compelling human need to believe - the need to be comforted - that easily clouds people's judgment. It's all too easy to fall into the seductive trap of a comforting fairy tale. So we resist, to the death, all explanations of the world based on anything but the Laws of Physics, mathematics and probability.[27]

Susskind doesn't go into any details as to why humans have a built-in need to *believe*, which explains the presence of religions in virtually every known human culture. I'm wondering if he has similar well-formed ideas about the compelling need of ambitious, aspiring scientists to develop original theories in their fields of research. How much are they willing to bend reality to set themselves apart from their colleagues? Admitting that God exists doesn't improve one's CV and certainly doesn't win research grants. But what if the world *was* indeed created? Can we afford to ignore such a momentous truth just because we don't currently have the instruments to study the implications of intelligent design? Our current scientific paradigm is indeed unable to deal with God, so perhaps we should rethink it. I'm obviously not qualified to suggest an alternative or even begin sketching a proposed solution. All I'm doing is pointing out the areas where science is more or less stuck: the origin of the universe and life, the complexity of molecular life, the mystery of consciousness. Of course, studying these topics using traditional scientific methods should continue. History is full of breakthroughs that followed apparent intellectual gridlocks. At the same time, since the more we discover about the universe, the more pronounced the appearance of intelligent design becomes, we should perhaps include other forms of knowledge in our quest to explain the world. The alternative of denying inconvenient facts can't bring any good. Stubbornly sticking to the same investigation methods won't help with concepts that don't fit into the scientific paradigm. Again, when all you have is a hammer, everything looks like a nail. Some fundamental truths require different approaches than those used in natural sciences over the last couple of centuries.

Let's use a scenario that I personally don't believe in, for reasons which will be covered later on, but which doesn't go against our current scientific understanding of the world. Imagine a computer-simulated reality (similar to open-world games such as Grand Theft Auto) in which the protagonists are conscious agents, intelligent enough to ask meaningful questions about life and the universe but unable to discover the true nature of their world, which ultimately consists of 1s and 0s. As time goes by, some characters will end up promoting the idea of a godless world based on inconclusive evidence, unaware of the computer hardware and the code that made their reality possible. Similarly, by denying the notion of a Creator, we as humans are turning our backs on the possibility that there might be a fundamental layer of reality that we're completely unaware of.

As in the case of a supernatural power who created the universe, the soul intuition is common across all cultures of the world. However, unlike the God intuition, which can be partially derived and explained by the principle of causality, the idea that each human being has an immaterial essence that transcends our earthly existence is actually counter-intuitive. Decrepitude, death, and decay are fundamental aspects of life. There are no rational arguments that can be made to support the notion of a soul. Of course, there are ways in which reality can be *interpreted* to construct a spiritual level of existence, but the afterlife can't be derived through logic. How can the idea of immortality arise in the absence of any proof to support it? According to some anthropologists, the notion of a soul appeared among primitive humans following their dreams, the trance states produced by either severe illness or consumption of hallucinogenic substances, and their reflections in surfaces of water. According to this theory, early humans must have concluded that there was a part of them lacking mass and volume that could roam the world and even talk to dead people while their bodies were asleep. It is a good starting point, but this explanation only goes halfway towards understanding the notion of the soul. The missing part is why we dream in the first place. As we shall see in chapter seven, dreams remain very much a mystery. Also, why do some people who understand the notions of deranged mental states, who know that reflections are nothing more than photons bouncing off surfaces and who ascribe dreams to the orchestrated firing of neurons still believe they have an immaterial self?

Another explanation is that the notion of an eternal soul originates in the need for human consolation. The world is a savage place, and we're condemned to an absurd existence from the day we are born. The idea of an eternal blissful existence beyond the physical realm is indeed appealing, and it even has the potential to make life more bearable. However, is the need for consolation sufficient to make humans actually *believe* there is such a thing as a soul? As Steve Pinker rightly observes about the consolation theory, self-deception can only go so far.

(...) it only raises the question of why a mind would evolve to find comfort in beliefs it can plainly see are false. A freezing person finds no comfort in believing he is warm; a person face-to-face with a lion is not put at ease by the conviction that it is a rabbit.[28]

Given that the concept of a soul is counter-intuitive and doesn't have any rational basis, it is paradoxical that it can be found in all cultures worldwide. What could be the explanation?

NEWTON'S MISSING LAW AND A PREBAKED GOD

One fundamental law of physics which Sir Isaac Newton never discovered, because he didn't have any children, states that any object within the proximity of two toddlers playing together is attracted with forces more or less equal by their tiny, unflinching hands, until one of them loses grip and finally bursts into tears. It's a law that any parent knows, and its explanation is deeply embedded in the human brain. Certain abstract concepts, such as the concepts of *ownership* or *being alive*, are pre-built structures in a child's mind. Once learned, the specific words for owning, keeping, or taking are simply assimilated into these structures, studies on infants have shown. Could it be possible that the concepts of *God* and *soul* are also pre-built mental structures, primitives that help us construct a model of the world? How else can we explain the presence of these notions in virtually all cultures scattered around the globe, from prehistoric times up to the modern-day?

Darwinists such as Richard Dawkins struggle to explain how evolutionary mechanisms could have possibly led to the prevalence of religions in all human cultures. Since religion is wasteful in terms of time and energy resources while having very little benefit to the survival of an individual's genes, how could natural selection have favored it? In *The God Delusion*, Dakins suggests that the roots of religion can be found in the obedient attitude children have toward their parents and tribal elders, which is valuable for survival.

> (...) the flip side of trusting obedience is slavish gullibility. The inevitable by-product is vulnerability to infection by mind viruses. For excellent reasons related to Darwinian survival, child brains need to trust parents, and elders whom parents tell them to trust. An automatic consequence is that the truster has no way of distinguishing good advice from bad. The child cannot know that "Don't paddle in the crocodile-infested Limpopo" is good advice but "You must sacrifice a goat at the time of the fool moon, otherwise the rains will fail" is at best a waste of time and goats. Both admonitions sound equally trustworthy. Both come from a respected source and are delivered with a solemn earnestness that commands respect and demands obedience. The same goes for propositions about the world, about the cosmos, about morality and about human nature. And, very likely, when the child grows up and has children of her own, she will naturally pass the whole lot on to her own children - nonsense as well as sense - using the same infectious gravitas of manner.[29]

I don't find Dawkins's explanation convincing at all. Children start to judge for themselves as they grow older and therefore are not condemned to have the same beliefs as their parents. In evolutionary terms, the individuals who can discern useful advice from useless superstitions have a greater chance to survive and reproduce, by keeping their goats and coming up with practical approaches for enduring droughts. Tendencies towards useless rituals and convictions will thus decline in future generations. Explaining why religions can be found in virtually every human culture is a challenging task. The ubiquity of spiritual beliefs points to something deeper than social phenomena such as obedience. It is as if the notions of God and soul are pre-built into the human brain, similarly to the concept of ownership. This would explain why the religion *meme*, to use a term coined by Richard Dawkins, is so highly successful in replicating. When religious beliefs enter a child's brain, they find a home already partially built for them. Religions and superstitions are derived from these two fundamental underlying mental structures, corresponding to the existence of a Creator and to a dualistic perception of the world. Dualists make a distinction between matter and mind and therefore believe they are more than just the sum of their body parts. And we are all natural-born dualists, the psychologist Paul Bloom has shown. Studies focused on young children have uncovered that humans have a pre-built common-sense dualism.

> *(...) while we have to learn the specific sort of afterlife that people in our culture believe in (heaven, reincarnation, spirit world, and so on), the notion that consciousness is separable from the body is not learned at all; it comes for free.*[30]

Through education and knowledge acquisition, we can unshackle ourselves from superstitions and religions, which have to be seen as byproducts of our inborn spiritual mental structures. However, we should avoid stifling the hard-wire intuitions that are part of our very own nature. Along with divine clues that have been put in place for us, which transform with every stage of our development as a species, they paint a picture of a universe that is a product of intelligent design.

Chapter 5

Consciousness and Free Will

FROM BATS TO PHILOSOPHICAL ZOMBIES

We intuitively feel that we know what consciousness is, but how can we define it? A good place to start is Thomas Nagel's paper "What is it Like to Be a Bat?". The American philosopher explains consciousness as *what it feels to be you*: "(...) an organism has conscious mental states if and only if there is something that it is like to *be* that organism -- something it is like *for* the organism."[31]

Pause for a second to notice how it *feels* like to be you right now. Your sense of vision allows you to read these words, and the meaning you derive from them triggers thoughts and emotions in your mind. Your attention is focused on this book, but you're still vaguely aware of your body and surroundings. If you look up, you can see the details of your environment and you can make sense of what's around you. In the present moment, your experience clearly has a subjective character.

Can you imagine how it would feel to be you if you were to become a bat? Of course, you can't, because it's simply not possible, as Nagel points out: "(...) if I try to imagine this, I am restricted to the resources of my own mind, and those resources are inadequate to the task." Our imagination is limited by our sensory abilities (we can see, hear, and smell, but not echolocate) and by the limited set of subjective experiences we've had so far. The phenomenon of

65

consciousness is also referred to as having the "lights on" or as someone being "at home," which is pretty obvious, especially if you imagine suddenly turning into a piece of furniture instead of a bat. Unlike inanimate objects, we can observe the world around us, and more importantly, extract meaning from it.

For modern science, mental states are the result of physical processes. Since human bodies are entirely made up of atoms, like all the other objects in the universe, there is nothing special about our brains, which are seen as highly advanced processing systems. For scientists, no distinction can be made between the mind and the brain. Therefore, consciousness is nowadays regarded as a byproduct, an emergent phenomenon of information processing. Why would information processing feel like something though? In his essay, Nagler admits that he has no idea: "The problem is unique. If mental processes are indeed physical processes, then there is something it is like, intrinsically, to undergo physical processes. What it is for such a thing to be the case remains a mystery".

Scientists fail to understand not only how consciousness is generated, but also why it is needed in the first place. Some believe that an alternate world with human beings lacking any sort of inner life would have been just as plausible, if not more probable, than the one we inhabit, in which every one of us has emotions and feelings. These imaginary creatures, which are identical in every way to humans, except that in their case "there's nobody home," are known as philosophical zombies. Daniel Dennett is one of the philosophers who believe that these theoretical zombies could be in principle possible, if technological advancements would allow us to create intelligent humanoid robots. They would speak and behave just like humans, but they would completely lack an inner life. Just as Richard Dawkins believes that God is a scientific problem, Dennett thinks that the problem of consciousness can only be interpreted in light of recent scientific discoveries, although little progress has actually been made so far.

Many theories have been proposed and what they have in common is the assumption that the function of consciousness is to aggregate and consolidate a multitude of information streams that reach the brain (what we see, what we hear, etc.). As computer science advanced in the second half of the century, the parallel with central processing units became inevitable. For example, Dennett compared sentience to a virtual machine[i]. Just as 19th-century scientists saw similarities between brains and steam engines, Dennett used the leading technology of that time to explain consciousness. However, his approach quickly proved unrealistic and somewhat naive, because the brain is unlike any computer that humans have built up to this point.

A single major analogy can be realistically made between brains and computers. Synaptic transmission is the brain function that is the most similar to the inner workings of a computer. It's targeted, binary and rapid. It involves passing messages between neurons across synapses, with the help of neurotransmitters, which can have either an inhibiting role or an exciting one. However, the synaptic transmission process is not intrinsically conscious. Moreover, the comparison between brains and computers stops here. From what we

---

[i] A virtual machine in the extended sense of the term, not to be confused with the technology for computer virtualization which became popular after 2005. "(...) almost any computer can be considered a virtual machine, since it is software - a systematic list of instructions - that, when it runs, turns a general purpose computer into a special-purpose machine that could have been designed and wired up as hardware." (Dennett, D. C. (2014) *Intuition Pumps*, Penguin Books, London, pp. 136-137)

currently know, the human brain is a sophisticated system orders of magnitude more complex than any technology that humans have built so far. It also operates on completely different principles than the sequential, deterministic Turing machines that pervade our technological lives. Therefore, explaining consciousness by relying on the brain-as-a-computer paradigm was a dead end to begin with.

CURIOSITY KILLED THE CONSCIOUS CAT

Following the pioneering work of Antonio Damasio, neuroscientists began to realize, at the end of the 20th century, that feelings and emotions are key for understanding the source of a person's true being. However, despite the progress made in the last two decades, science still can't explain how matter becomes mind and how thoughts and feelings turn into physical actions. The most promising theory we have at the moment, proposed by the neuroscientist Mark Solms, is that consciousness serves the biological function of *feeling our way* when confronted with unexpected circumstances, by enabling voluntary actions. The example Solms uses in his book *The Hidden Spring* is a person who realizes that the level of oxygen is decreasing in a room. Every cognitive resource is suddenly focused on restoring the organism's ability to breathe, by *feeling* the way through the problem: go to another room, check for windows that could be opened, etc. The effects of each action are compared against the organisms' registered states (in this particular case, the sensation of suffocation). This is how we evaluate our actions as effective or useless. How can you have a feeling without feeling it? asks Solms, who defines our sentient experience as a moment-by-moment sense of how well we are doing, no matter what we're involved in.

According to Solms's theory, not all situations can be handled by resorting to instinctive reactions, even if these are "preferred" by the brain on account of being more energy-efficient. Anything that can be automated is automated, but instinctive reactions are not enough for complex organisms. Jumping for fear when you see a snake on the ground is done with no perceptual consciousness, but more complex scenarios, which bring conditions of uncertainty, require higher-order thinking and, implicitly, a state of subjective being. Therefore, consciousness is the realm of the non-automatable.

Alongside five modalities of perceptual consciousness (sight, hearing, taste, smell, and touch), which evolved to qualify different categories of external information that are registered by our sensory organs, the neuroscientist identifies seven varieties of affective consciousness, which qualify different categories of emotional needs in *all mammals*: lust, seeking, rage, fear, panic/grief, care, and play. Of all seven, *seeking* deserves special attention, since it is the only one that *proactively* engages with uncertainty. It is also our default emotion, which manifests itself as a generalized sense of interest in the world.

> *SEEKING[i] generates exploratory "foraging behaviour", accompanied by a conscious feeling state that may be characterised as expectancy, interest, curiosity, enthusiasm or optimism. Think of a dog in an open field: no matter what its current bodily needs are, foraging propels it to engage positively with the environment, so that it might satisfy them there.[32]*

---

[i] Solms capitalizes the terms for basic emotions to emphasize that he is referring to whole brain functions, not just feelings.

The benefits of including feelings and emotions in a theory of consciousness are undeniable; however, Solms's theory does leave some fundamental questions unanswered. First and foremost, it does not explain how physical reactions in the brain actually produce the experience of consciousness. Moreover, even though Solms asserts that consciousness is the product of an evolutionary process, his explanation for how such a process would have looked in reality is sketchy at best.

> *(...) I imagine the dawn of life in one of those hydro-thermal vents. The unicellular organisms that came into being there would surely not have been conscious, but their survival prospects would have been affected by their ambient surrounds. It is easy to imagine these simple organisms responding to the biological "goodness" of the energy of the sun. From there, it is a small step to imagine more complex creatures actively striving for such energy supplies and eventually evolving a capacity to weigh the chances of success by alternative actions.[33]*

At a closer look, the "small step" that Solms refers to is in fact a giant leap. Even if a feeling of "goodness" for the Sun's energy were to arise in a primitive organism, an instinctive *follow-the-heat* mechanism would have been enough to capitalize on it. Complex cognitive processes, such as deciding between multiple courses of action, rely on subjective states. These initial conscious states only had corresponding trial-and-error behaviors, so they couldn't possibly have been naturally selected. They did not provide any reproductive advantage. In the context of complex organisms, there is also the question of why doesn't the state of consciousness disappear when there is no need for actions based on high-level reasoning? After all, the preferred state of the brain is an unconscious one, on account of the higher energy consumption required by sentience. Solms's solution of the default *seeking* emotional need is questionable in evolutionary terms. We all know that curiosity killed the cat. The risk of engaging with the environment is often higher than the benefits of the potential learning experiences it brings. The fact that consciousness is never put on pause highlights a more fundamental role than voluntary behavior in unexpected circumstances. Solms's great triumph is that he was able to translate his theory into a mathematical model. His achievement has been seen as an important step in proving that consciousness is exclusively the product of physical processes in the brain. However, nothing has been proven yet, so the mind-body duality promoted for centuries remains a valid alternative.

CONSCIOUSNESS − PHYSICAL REALITY = GOD

The reductionist, materialist, and deterministic view of the mind is a modern approach, born from the scientific desire to predict the mechanisms of consciousness, even if only probabilistically. In opposition, the *mind-body dualism* theory, which originated in ancient times and was refined by the Dutch philosopher René Descartes in the 17th century, claims that the mind and the body are separate entities. For Descartes, humans are a combination of mind and body, which are closely joined and yet extremely different. Cartesian dualism influenced Western philosophy for centuries and continues to remain valid for many people, including members of the scientific community. In the second half of the 20th century, based on discoveries in the fields of physiology and neuroscience, scientists started to suggest that the mind-body distinction is wrong and that the mind can be reduced entirely to the functions of the brain. However, the notion that consciousness is nothing more than the orchestrated firing of neurons is deeply counter-intuitive. Reductionists have put a lot of effort into promoting a purely biological substrate of consciousness. In 2005, the journal *Science* ranked the top 125 open questions in science, and "What is the universe made of?" came first. The runner-up was "What is the biological basis of consciousness?", a question that reveals a strong bias, as the cognitive psychologist Douglas Hoffman shows in his book *The Case Against Reality*. Researchers hope and expect that there is a biological basis for consciousness, but this could be nothing more than wishful thinking, as Hoffman points out.

> *We have no scientific theories that explain how brain activity - or computer activity, or any other kind of physical activity - could cause, or be, or somehow give rise to, conscious experience. We don't have even one idea that's remotely plausible. If we consider not just brain activity, but also the complex interactions among brains, bodies and the environment, we still strike out. We're stuck. Our utter failure leads some to call this the 'hard problem' of consciousness, or simply a "mystery."*[34]

Hoffman's way out of this intellectual conundrum is to dismiss reality altogether. He argues that space and time are mere illusions and that reality can be reduced to conscious agents interacting with one another. By getting rid of the physical universe completely, Hoffman was able to create a mathematical model which describes not only the concept of consciousness but even God, seen as an infinite conscious agent. Some of Hoffman's fellow scientists objected to his theory because it puts humans at the center of everything, which, as we have seen, must be avoided at all cost, following the Ptolemaic fiasco. However, in my opinion, the real weak point is the complete repudiation of reality for the sake of translating sentience into mathematical equations. Hoffman stretches consciousness to the point where objective reality breaks down. Without a physical reality that exists in the absence of conscious observers, a simple experience such as navigating through a dark room filled with obstacles becomes an ontological predicament. Since you're under no influence from other conscious agents when bumping into various objects, the only remaining option is a self-fabricated perception of your surroundings, as random as the contents of dreams. The patterns and predictability that characterize real life would disappear completely if Hoffman's theory were to be true. If his radical approach proves something, it's that the dissolution of reality is too high a price to pay for the benefit of mathematically modeling consciousness.

ENSLAVING FREE WILL

In a series of studies conducted in the 1980s, the physiologist Benjamin Libet seemingly demonstrated that electrical activity built up in the participants' brains before they consciously decided to move. Over the following decades, other research programs consolidated Libet's findings, to the point where modern neuroscience considers free will to be nothing more than an illusion. It would seem that all our intentions and actions are triggered in unconscious parts of the brain, which we don't have access to. The impression that we are somehow in control is just self-deception. Our conscious experience is just a phantasm of authority. All we do is continuously fool ourselves by trying to interpret, justify and explain the inscrutable decisions made in the darkest corners of our brains, which we can't control and have no way to access. Even though several problematic issues have been pointed out later on concerning Libet's experiments, the notion of an illusory free will kept growing in popularity. As it has been shown, subjective awareness of self-decision making is unreliable, so participants can't accurately identify the precise moment when they decide to move a body part. Moreover, ensuing disagreements between researchers highlighted that there is no clear consensus on what the electrical activity in the participants' brains actually reflects. Despite all these weak points, the scientific temptation to get rid of free will was just too great. Since the mind can be reduced to particle interactions and particles are governed by the laws of physics, free will can't exist since our brains are entirely deterministic constructs. In theory, all our thoughts and actions could be known in advance, if only science could map a perfect physical model of the brain. This means that if it were somehow possible to put a person in the same exact situation a million times, their thoughts, emotions, decisions, and actions would be identical each time.

Science can't possibly accept the concept of free will. After explaining physical phenomena at all scales, from the forces responsible for keeping atoms together to the motions of galaxies, by translating them into elegant mathematical equations, science's next goal is to do the same for living organisms. Modern physics can mathematically describe grandiose cosmic events, but can't do the same for seemingly prosaic entities, such as bacteria. The ultimate goal is to discover equations for all complex systems, including humans, and this is why free will can't be tolerated. If we accept that the material world can be shaped and influenced by phenomena sourced from the realm of thoughts and ideas, science loses its ability to predict everything, even if only probabilistically. This is the real reason behind the scientific attempt to dismiss free will as a mere illusion.

Chapter 6

The Purpose of the Universe

DON'T FORGET ABOUT THE USERS

Like many failed projects in the IT industry, the evolutionism vs. creationism debates touching on the topic of *design* have left out completely one key aspect: the *users*. From William Paley's watch to Michael Behe's mousetrap, the focus has been exclusively on the end products resulting from the design process. However, I believe the users, seen as intentional agents, are just as important.

In Paley's example, the user is the person trying to tell the time by looking at the watch. In Behe's case, someone who is waging war against rodents. Users are key to understanding the overall design process, because a good design will always anticipate their *expectations*. We can expand on this idea and assert that a system designed to provide functionality for users always has a *purpose*. A good design matches the designer's *intentions* on how the system is meant to be used to achieve its *purpose* (functionality) with the users' *expectations* regarding what they need to do to achieve their *goals*. To summarize, a system designed for user interactions has a *purpose* and reflects the designer's *intentions*. As for the users, they have *goals* and *expectations*.

I will use smartphones as an example instead of watches and mousetraps because I will need to use the concept of *user interface* in my argument. I have referred to the first iPhone in the introduction of this book. It was a great success because

77

the design intentions fully matched the users' expectations. The interface between the system and the users met this principle and as a result, the gadget industry realized that the era of user manuals was over. Smartphones do a lot more than just phone calls, but for the sake of clarity, I'm going to limit myself to this single function. Let's see how a smartphone reflects the main aspects of a designed system:

System: Mobile phone

Purpose: Allow users to make phone calls

Designer's intention: Users will figure out what pictograms to touch in order to make phone calls just by looking at the screen

Users' expectation: Make phone calls by following the relevant pictograms displayed on the screen (in this case, starting from the icon depicting a phone receiver)

Users' goal: Make phone calls

We can see that it is possible to figure out the *purpose* of a well-designed system by starting from the users' *goals*. We can follow the process using the previous examples: the purpose of a watch is to tell the time, while the owner's goal is to find out what time it is. The purpose of a mousetrap is to kill mice, while the buyer's goal is to get rid of them. Returning to smartphones, the user interface can tell a lot about the design process. I'm using a successful example, but for each efficient design, many others fail to meet the users' expectations. When the design intentions anticipate and match the user expectations, we have the mark of good design.

THE USER – DESIGNED SYSTEM DUALITY OF THE HUMAN BEING

I hope I was successful so far in showing that there is enough evidence all around us to prove that the universe is the product of an intelligent Designer. Furthermore, I do believe in evolution from a common ancestor, but one that has been planned to result in the appearance of our species. Based on these assumptions, I will proceed to apply the same user-based design analysis as we did for a smartphone to the concept of a designed universe, in order to identify its purpose. Before we proceed, it is crucial to understand that humans are not just users of the universe (seen as an overarching system), but also sub-systems that have been designed in their turn. As intentional agents with the ability to pursue our goals, we interact with the universe using a truly amazing interface that has been provided to us, the human mind. At the same time, we are an integral part of the world we live in, subsystems that bear the indisputable mark of design. Our purpose as designed systems is the one given to us by God, and it's identical to our main goal. Let's see what this goal is, using the viewpoint of *humans as users of the universe.*

Individually, humans have a multitude of goals, ranging from simply staying alive to finding meaning through love, from petty power struggles to passing our genes to the next generations. However, if we look back at our collective evolution as a species, throughout millennia, a clear pattern emerges: humanity has struggled, using more or less inspired approaches, to figure out the origin of the universe and the meaning of life. We have been constantly driven by a feeling of unquenchable curiosity to push the boundaries of knowledge in the hope that we might ultimately discover fundamental truths. Humanity's goal is to discover God. Scientism might prefer to formulate it differently, referring to "fundamental laws" of the universe instead, but the principle is the same. Now that we've identified that the human species, seen collectively as a group of users, has the ultimate goal of discovering God, we can move on to identify what our primary expectation is: studying the world will expand our knowledge and unravel fundamental truths about the universe.

We might feel entitled to expect answers to the questions we're asking, but, in fact, this is not really the case. As we have seen in chapter four, "the eternal mystery of the world is its comprehensibility," as Einstein beautifully formulated it. We should be amazed that we're able to discover the laws and principles that govern our universe. This is not a given or a simple coincidence. It is a gift. The unreasonable effectiveness of mathematics in natural sciences suggests that the interface we use to interact with the universe, the human mind, has been purposefully designed to meet our expectations as users. Therefore, the designer's intention was for us to be able to comprehend the mechanisms of the system we're a part of. The helpful clues that have been customized for each stage of our development as a species strengthen the argument of a carefully designed interface.

We can now summarize our progress so far:

System: The universe
Purpose: ???
Designer's intention: Users will be able to figure out answers to their fundamental questions, by using their built-in reasoning capacities and the deliberate clues provided to them

Users' expectation: Studying the world will expand our knowledge and allow us to discover fundamental truths about the universe and its Creator

Users' goal: Discover God

The only task left is to identify the purpose of the system. You might have already figured it out by now. The purpose of the universe is to allow its users to discover God. It seems that the universe is a giant puzzle that we have to solve collectively as sentient, intelligent members of the human species, by gradually expanding our knowledge. What awaits us at the end is still a mystery. Since our goals are identical to our purpose as designed systems, the journey seems to be what matters most.

Chapter 7

Afterlife

OUR DAILY ACTS OF RESURRECTION

The *Epic of Gilgamesh*, the world's oldest recorded story, focuses on the adventures of a Mesopotamian king on a quest to find immortality. After many dangerous undertakings, he is challenged to stay awake for six days and seven nights, but fails to do so. As a result, he wastes his chance of becoming immortal. We can see that a correlation between death and sleep has been made since ancient times. Sleep is the daily image of death, but at the same awakenings are symbolic acts of resurrection. From the moment we are born, we figuratively die and are brought back to life every single day.

What's even more amazing is what happens between going to sleep and waking up. We lie down with our eyes closed, and after a while, we're magically transported to fantastic realms in which everything is possible. You can fly, you can become another person or even an animal, you can talk to dead people. Anything is possible and everything goes. The role of sleep is still a mystery, even though many theories have been proposed. It has been suggested that dreams are imaginary simulation scenarios with cathartic effects, to prepare us for distressful real-life events. Or perhaps they're meant to regulate our emotions by allowing us to act our wildest impulses free from the inhibitions of the wakeful state. Nobody really knows. Since all we have are speculations, I will allow myself to put forward one of my own: dreams are a form of knowledge. They inform us that other states of consciousness can be achieved, independent of rational causality and coercive social norms. Dreams are a window to another world, made up entirely of pure feelings and emotions. They are preparing us for the journey that lies ahead.

HOW TECHNOLOGY MADE AFTERLIFE POSSIBLE

Until not very long ago, science would have vehemently denied the possibility of an afterlife. There's no place for a soul when humans are exclusively made out of atoms, reason dictates. Antony Flew's "conversion" from atheism to deism illustrates how someone can believe in God based on scientific grounds and at the same time fail to acknowledge the possibility of an afterlife. In 2004, the British philosophy professor known for his atheist views up to that point announced that he had changed his mind and started believing in an intelligent Creator of the universe. In a book published three years later, *There is a God,* Flew explained that he reconsidered his position on God's existence based on recent scientific discoveries.

> *I now believe that the universe was brought into existence by an infinite Intelligence. I believe that this universe's intricate laws manifest what scientists have called the Mind of God. I believe that life and reproduction originate in a divine Source (...) Why do I believe this, given that I expounded and defended atheism for more than a half century? The short answer is this: this is the world picture, as I see*

it, that has emerged from modern science. Science spotlights three dimensions of nature that point to God. The first is the fact that nature obeys laws. The second is the dimension of life, of intelligently organized and purpose-driven beings, which arose from matter. The third is the very existence of nature.[35]

In the ensuing controversy, some claimed that his advanced age (he was 81 one at the time of the announcement) caused him to change his mind. Flew denied that his conversion was triggered by his fear of dying and made it clear that while he started believing in God, he remained convinced that there was no afterlife. Two decades earlier, in his book *The Logic of Mortality*, the philosophy professor had identified three possibilities of survival after death, by summarizing the history of religious and philosophical thought: a resurrection-type event, with dead people regaining their flesh and bones bodies they once possessed, the existence of "astral bodies" and the existence of souls. The distinction between the last two is that the former have corporeal characteristics, while the latter do not. Flew dismissed all three possibilities, concluding that there cannot be an afterlife.

However, in the current digital age that we live in, the concept of an afterlife is no longer logically and scientifically impossible. By combining the developments made in the last decades in the fields of computing and neuroscience, a new theory emerged: we might live in a simulated world. If the human mind can be reduced to nothing more than information processing, then it means that we could very well populate a virtual reality. Even more so, the probability that we live in a simulated universe is very high, according to the simulation hypothesis put forward by the philosopher Nick Bostrom. Since a highly advanced, post-human civilization will have enormous computing power and will be able to run detailed simulations of their ancestors, we are likely part of a simulation, unless all civilizations self-destruct before they reach the ability to run these simulations or they simply choose not to do so, for reasons we can only speculate on (ethical considerations, for example). The simulation hypothesis opens up a whole new world of possibilities, no matter who created our simulated world. It could be a high school hacker from the year 10,000 or even an alien civilization. If we do live in a simulated digital universe, death could be compared to the beginning of a new level in a video game. Materialists can't disagree, since this is in line with the laws of physics.

We can even take this theory a step further for the sake of proving that literally anything is possible. If we can inhabit a simulated universe, why not a generated *variation* of the actual universe? Maybe in the real one, Richard Dawkins is a vicar and publishes best-selling books on Christian angelology. If the totality of our experiences can be reduced to the code behind a simulated reality, death could very well be the beginning of a new iteration. Consciousness and a sense of identity could be maintained. Nothing needs to be reconstructed because nothing is destroyed. No mysterious substance, such as the soul, is required.

IN THE BEGINNING, GOD CREATED
THE CPU AND THE RAM

Ultimately, what if the *real* universe is nothing more than a virtual world? If we expand on the simulated universe theory, we realize that God didn't actually have to build a full-scale physical universe. A series of 1s and 0s and the capacity to run this binary code would have been enough to achieve the same result. As a dualist, who believes that the mind is more than the combined functions of the brain, I find the idea of a digitally generated universe unnecessarily complicated. In line with Occam's Razor principle, a created world is a simpler and better explanation. However, I'm attracted to the simulation hypothesis as a useful thought experiment for highlighting the implications entailed by the existence of an intelligent Designer. Let's linger a bit more in the realm of this logically and physically possible virtual world that we potentially live in. What if its Creator provided us deliberate, inconspicuous clues about his presence and the meaning of our existence? Knowledge means both facts and clues, depending if a particular truth is known in advance or not. Facts could possibly mean something if someone were to somehow connect the dots, but the overall ambiguity means that deriving meaning is highly improbable. On the other hand, clues are what make detective stories so appealing. Many times, they are the only option for elucidating an initially known mystery. All facts are potential clues, it just takes a discerning eye to identify them. One by one, they bring new perspectives, enhance our overall understanding and trigger a re-evaluation of everything that was known up to that point. Taken individually they might be worthless, but put together they have remarkable demystifying power.

By focusing exclusively on studying the subsystems of the universe and the way they interact with one another - the approach that modern science is based on -, the trail of crumbs left behind by the Creator will be missed. Without a higher level of meaning, which transcends the physical world, humanity will forever remain baffled by the regularity of our universe, from the fine-tuning of its structure without which life would not have been possible to the unreasonable effectiveness of mathematics in the natural sciences. Even if science could describe in minute details the totality of particle interactions in the universe, the patterns behind them would remain meaningless and undecipherable. A different approach is needed, which involves a teleological (a fancy philosophical word for purpose-oriented) analysis of new scientific discoveries as potential clues to unravel the mystery of the Designer of the universe. If we look close enough, we'll start to see that there are deliberate clues that have been left for us, and they've been pointing to the same "suspect" all along.

This is by no means a new idea. In fact, the belief that the principles of physics are not enough to adequately explain the universe was a tenet of the Age of Enlightenment, which laid out the foundation of modern science. The polymath Gottfried Wilhelm Leibnitz, one of the most prominent figures of the Enlightenment, argued that the ultimate reason for all things is God. He saw a finalism in living beings, which falls under an overarching finalism of the world.

> *Anyone who sees the admirable structure of animals will find himself forced to recognize the wisdom of the author of things. And I advise those who have any feelings of piety and even feelings of true philosophy to keep away from the phrases of certain would-be freethinkers who say that we see because it happens that we have eyes and not that eyes were made for seeing.*[36]

For Leibnitz, the ultimate reason for all things is God, and he proposed that all scientific endeavors should be made to decipher this final cause. In other words, the purpose of studying nature should be to figure out *the meaning of it all*. He proposed that investigating the mechanisms of the universe should be combined with efforts to decipher the fundamental purpose behind all natural phenomena: "Both ways are good and both can be useful, not only for admiring the skill of the Great Worker, but also for discovering something useful in physics and in medicine."[37] Leibnitz's contemporary, Sir Isaac Newton, asserted that the laws of motion that govern celestial bodies, which he discovered, were the work of a skilled Creator. "This most beautiful System of the Sun, Planets and Comets, could only proceed from the counsel and dominion of an intelligent and powerful being. (...) This Being governs all things, not as the soul of the world, but as Lord over all: And on account of his dominion he is wont to be called *Lord God* παντοκράτωρ or *Universal Ruler*. (...) The supreme God is a Being eternal, infinite, absolutely perfect", he wrote in *Philosophiae Naturalis Principia Mathematica*, probably the most important scientific work ever published. We can see that science started with God as the ultimate cause for every natural phenomenon. It was obvious to the great thinkers of the Age of Reason that the grandeur of all creation could only be explained in supernatural terms. The world is too well put together to be a product of chance.

Modern science has lost this sense of wonder and modesty. With every new discovery, the feeling of intellectual arrogance grew stronger and stronger, replacing the attitude of humility in front of God's creation. After all, the *mechanisms of the parts* can be explained very well without having a holistic view that includes the Designer who created them in the first place. In time, as religions have been unmasked as man-made and Darwin's theory of evolution through natural selection rose to prominence, it started to look like the only possible modern God was a non-intervening one, reduced to a merely "ceremonial" role of triggering the unfolding of the universe. Therefore, studying the implication of his presence is now considered a pointless exercise, since our scientific tools are unable to test the hypothesis of an intelligent Designer. Even though science has highlighted the moment of Creation, in the form of the Big Bang, the progress made in the field of quantum mechanics has led some physicists to believe that God can be completely removed from the picture and that the universe supposedly came into existence by itself, just as life did.

Over the last centuries, we went from the God-centric beliefs of the Enlightenment thinkers to the godless views of modern atheist scientists, who believe that they're capable of understanding everything and who proclaim that the universe was created from *nothing*. Today's scientists are guided by a feeling of unbounded confidence in their ability to decipher the origin and inner workings of life and the universe, without having to take into account an intelligent Designer. "To succumb to the God Temptation in either of those guises, biological or cosmological, is an act of intellectual capitulation," boasts Richard Dawkins, while the cosmologist and theoretical physicists Lawrence Krauss announces there is no longer a need to discover the "why": "invoking 'God' to avoid difficult questions of 'how' is merely intellectually lazy." These two views are representative of the mainstream scientific consensus: there is no need for a Creator to explain either the origin of the universe or the appearance of life.

Moreover, Richard Dawkins, probably the most arrogant and aggressive apostle of atheism, even goes as far as to compare himself with the Creator of the universe. The biologist refutes the claim that God, seen as a single, ultimate cause, is a *simple* explanation for the existence of the universe, by fallaciously extending this simplicity to the Creator himself, in order to deny it. In the process, he unwittingly depicts God almost as his intellectual rival.

> *[God] has to be clever enough to calculate, with exquisite and prophetic precision, the exact values of the physical constants that would fine-tune a universe to yield, 13.8 billion years later, a species capable of worshipping him. You call that simple? At the same time, in his singular simplicity, he had to foresee that the nuclear force must be set 10^{36} times stronger than gravity; and he had to calculate with similar exactitude the precisely requisite values of half a dozen critical numbers, the fundamental constants in physics. You and I possess prodigiously complex brains evolved over hundreds of millions of years, but do you understand quantum mechanics? I certainly don't. Yet God, that paragon of ultimate pure simplicity, not only understands it but invented it. Plus Special and General Relativity. Plus the Higgs boson and dark matter.[38]*

Fast forward a thousand, ten thousand, or even a million years, Dawkins's enumeration will undoubtedly include many other fields of knowledge that God would have to master and that humans are completely unaware of. How can we be sure that the new layers of complexity that we are bound to uncover will not change our perception of divinity? Some people thrive in complexity, fearing that simple solutions could diminish their inflated egos. Paradoxically, the transition from perceiving the world as the work of a skillful Creator to the modern viewpoint of *everything from nothing* is not based on facts. Ultimately, there are still many unknowns. There are no demonstrations for how the universe or life started, only assumptions. Declaring God unnecessary was done in haste and needs to be reconsidered. There are still a lot of holes in our understanding of reality, starting with what reality actually is.

THE CASE AGAINST REALITY

The simulation hypothesis is not the only scientifically valid theory that permits the existence of an afterlife. As we have seen earlier, the cognitive psychologist Donald Hoffman has put forward a theory in which space and time are mere illusions, and reality is reduced to multiple conscious agents interacting with one another. In his book, Hoffman starts by arguing that the laws of natural selection made us perceive reality not as it truly is, but in a distorted way, which enhanced our ability to survive from an evolutionary perspective, despite its lack of representational accuracy. According to Hoffman, spacetime is not the fundamental component of the universe, as modern physics states in accordance with the general theory of relativity. Instead, space and time are structures that *we* create as conscious agents, by observing and interacting with reality, which is, in fact, unlike anything that we perceive. Just as a digital picture saved on a computer desktop is nothing more than a representation of a long series of bits encoded on a data storage device, the physical properties of the world around us are just interfaces for the true nature of the universe. Hoffman draws a parallel to a video game such as Grand Theft Auto. The true building blocks of the game are not the pixels that make up the characters and the virtual reality which they inhabit, but processor states and bits stored in memory.

Hoffmans ends up taking his theory a step further and asserts that the objects around us, such as the Moon and Sun, supposedly exist only if an observer perceives them. They don't exist in themselves, because the world consists of nothing else than conscious experiences and conscious agents interacting with one another. Hoffman's theory, which he calls the conscious agent thesis, covers both the concept of God and the possibility of an afterlife. God is an infinite conscious agent, with unlimited potential for experiences, decisions, and actions. Death could mean just a change in how we perceive the true nature of reality.

> *Suppose you drive with friends to a virtual-reality arcade to play volleyball. You slip on headsets and body suits, and find your avatars clad in swimsuits, immersed in sunshine, standing on a sandy beach with a volleyball net, surrounded by swaying palms and crying gulls. You serve the ball and start playing with abandon. After a while, one of your friends says he's thirsty and will be right back. He slips out of his headset and body suit. His avatar collapses onto the sand, inert and unresponsive. But he's fine. He just stepped out of the virtual-reality interface.*[39]

I personally don't find Hoffman's thesis convincing, because God is ultimately a much simpler explanation for the mystery of consciousness. However, his original approach to the fundamental nature of reality shows us that we should avoid dismissing *anything* based on current scientific evidence, especially relating to the most profound and mysterious aspects of life. Science is not a model of the universe, it's a method of inquiry, and the fundamental truths it presents us are constantly changing. What doesn't make sense and is deemed impossible today ends up being unanimously accepted tomorrow. In this chapter, I've presented two flavors of immortality compatible with modern science, in the context in which only a couple of decades ago, the notion of an afterlife would have been considered intellectually ludicrous. There is still so much we don't understand. Science's victories against religions in the last centuries have been easy wins. We shouldn't let arrogance get the best of us and claim that the small scientific[i] successes we had so far entitle us to believe that we already have all the answers for the great mysteries of existence: the origin of the universe, the emergence of life and the miracle of consciousness. We have a lot more to discover.

---

[i] As stated previously, I'm not trying to belittle the scientific progress achieved so far or the difficulty of attaining it. I'm just highlighting that there's a lot more to be achieved and that *Homo Scientificus* is still cooing in a cradle.

Chapter 8

Infinitely Evil

THE ILLUSION OF PAIN

What kind of God would allow children to suffer? He either doesn't exist, or he's downright evil. Fyodor Dostoevsky's masterpiece *The Karamazov Brothers* brilliantly illustrates this argument, known as the problem of evil, when the character Ivan invokes the sufferings of a five-year-old girl tortured by her own parents.

> *Can you understand why a little creature, who can't even understand what's done to her, should beat her little aching heart with her tiny fist in the dark and the cold, and weep her meek unresentful tears to dear, kind God to protect her? Do you understand that, friend and brother, you pious and humble novice? Do you understand why this infamy must be and is permitted? Without it, I am told, man could not have existed on earth, for he could not have known good and evil. Why should he know that diabolical good and evil when it costs so much? Why, the whole world of knowledge is not worth that child's prayer to "dear, kind God!" I say nothing of the sufferings of grown-up people, they have eaten the apple, damn them, and the devil take them all! But these little ones! (...) Tell me yourself, I challenge you*

> *- answer. Imagine that you are creating a fabric of human destiny with the object of making men happy in the end, giving them peace and rest at last, but that it was essential and inevitable to torture to death only one tiny creature - that baby beating its breast with its fist, for instance - and to found that edifice on its unavenged tears, would you consent to be the architect on those conditions?*[40]

Of course, the suffering of innocent beings is terrible, but at a closer look, the so-called "problem of evil" is, in fact, not a problem at all. Ivan's argument is simply based on our inability to think at a cosmic scale. If there is an afterlife, we can't possibly begin to imagine what awaits us on the other side. The range of potential feelings and emotions, from extreme suffering to ecstatic joy, could be billions of times wider than what we can experience as human beings here on Earth. At such a scale, a lifetime of human pain and suffering would be nothing more than a meaningless blip. Before the modern principles of parenting and hi-tech dentistry, it wasn't something for parents to forcefully immobilize their children during painful procedures, such as tooth extractions. If we were to judge parents based solely on their behavior during such traumatic events, we would surely depict them as monsters. Of course, our understanding changes if we take into account their good intentions, the pain of having to see their children suffering, and the context of an entire lifetime of parental love and care. We shouldn't judge someone based on a single hour of their life, and we shouldn't use a human lifetime to judge God. We can't understand why there is suffering in the world; however, God and an eternal afterlife can make it completely meaningless. Seen from such an angle, the problem of evil is actually *a paradox of evil*: someone refuses to believe in God not because they find the concepts of soul and afterlife to be preposterous, but on account of the evil that exists in the world. And yet, if there is a Creator *everything* is possible, including a range of post-human emotions and experiences so vast that make our earthly lives insignificant in the grand scheme of things, no matter how blessed or wretched we currently think we are.

It's like waking up from a long dream and realizing that all those events happened in just a couple of seconds, while we briefly dozed off. We don't lament the agony we sometimes experience in our dreams, because it becomes trivial in the context of the state of consciousness we experience while awake (what we call reality). Imagine a post-reality of a higher order, in which our terrestrial life spans would equate to nothing more than the twinkling of an eye. How would we look back on the evil of the world, if at all?

HOW WOULD A CREATED UNIVERSE LOOK LIKE?

For thousands of years, humans have looked up at the sky and felt crushingly small. Failing to properly understand the world around them, they've ascribed divine qualities to celestial bodies. As our scientific understanding of the world progressed, the Moon, the Sun, and the planets have lost their godly status. We eventually understood that the universe is far bigger than the sum of the stars visible with the naked eye. Racing to build more powerful and better-positioned telescopes, so we can peer farther and farther into the depths of the universe, we rarely pause to ponder *why* the universe is so big and what are the implications of its immensity. Contemplating the vastness of the universe, the magnitude of wasted space and matter becomes deeply troubling, especially when we consider that it's very likely that we're the only intelligent species. Given that the universe is expanding so rapidly and that the speed of light is finite, there are stars so far away from us that their light will never reach us. This is how vast the cosmos is.

Let's do another variation of the thought experiment from the second chapter. Imagine being born in a universe no bigger than our planetary system, surrounded by an inscrutable edge where the laws of physics would break down. Science would confirm that crossing this barrier or finding out what's behind it is impossible. What metaphysical implications would such a world have? Could it be possible that the vastness of the universe we inhabit is meant to remind us that we're part of something bigger? Something so big that it's impossible not to feel humbled. The magnitude of our world inspires us to expand our thinking to cosmic scales. It's the interpretation key for our ephemeral condition. It's as if the universe is telling us that there is so much more out there waiting for us. Of course, the exact opposite could be argued: the vastness of the universe illustrates our irrelevance and meaningless. We inhabit an ordinary planet in a random corner of the universe, and our existential footprint amounts to nothing more than a drop in the cosmic ocean. These two opposing views highlight the limitation of science. It can present facts about the universe, such as its size, but it leaves out the fundamental *whys*. The observable universe has a diameter of 93 billion light-years, according to modern estimations, but what are we to make of this immensity? It's all down to interpretation, to meanings we as humans derive from objective facts. Since meanings are outside the reach of science, we're only left with subjective experiences.

Atheists such as Richard Dawkins like to oppose themselves to religious fundamentalists by saying that they're willing to change their views on the existence of God based on new evidence. It's not clear what kind of evidence they realistically expect to come their way though. Do they hope for a mathematical demonstration of divinity, a God equation? Or maybe find a God subatomic watermark that permeates the structure of the universe? "Tell me, why do people always say that it was natural for men to assume that the Sun went around the Earth rather than the Earth was rotating?" Ludwig Wittgenstein once challenged a friend. The reply was prompt: "Well, obviously, because it just looks as if the Sun is going around the Earth". "Well, what would it look like if it had looked as if the Earth were rotating?" retorted the philosopher. In the same spirit, we can ask the atheists who dismiss God for lack of evidence: "What would it look like if the universe was created?" The evidence is all around us, it only takes a change of perspective to see it.

Unfortunately, for some hardcore atheists, changing their minds is no longer an option, and they openly admit it. It is the case of chemist Robert Shapiro, who used a hypothetical scenario to illustrate his unwavering dedication to the scientific method, despite all else.

> *Some future day may yet arrive when all reasonable chemical experiments run to discover a probable origin for life have failed unequivocally. Further, new geological evidence may indicate a sudden appearance of life on the earth. Finally, we may have explored the universe and found no trace of life, or process leading to life, elsewhere. In such a case, some scientists might choose to turn to religion for an answer. Others, however, myself included, would attempt to sort out the surviving less probable scientific explanations in the hope of selecting one that was still more likely than the remainder.[41]*

Scientific truths about the fundamental facts of our universe don't mean anything by themselves unless they're interpreted. As long as these interpretations oppose the possibility that the world was created by an intelligent Designer, his existence will never be *proved*. I've tried to highlight the most obvious examples in the previous chapters. We know that the universe had a beginning, but the scientific *interpretation* (based on personal preference, not on facts) is that the Big Bang is just an ordinary cosmic event. The universe is fine-tuned for the existence of life, but the *interpretation* is that this is just a coincidence and there must be other universes that are not as life-friendly as our own. Science hasn't been able to demonstrate that life can just emerge from primordial soups of inorganic matter, yet the statistical assumption is that it must have happened as a result of fortuitous particle interactions over millions of years.

CUSTOM-MADE SUFFERING

Going back to Ivan Karamazov, to fully understand his predicament, we need to take a closer look at the concept of suffering. Without advocating a view that denies the existence of anything but one's mind, known in philosophy as solipsism, we should be wary of labeling God as evil based entirely on other people's tribulations. The feeling of suffering is a subjective, conscious experience, with clearly demarcated boundaries which surround one's self. Such *qualia* (the philosophical term for these subjective experiences) are fundamentally personal and can't be transmitted between individuals, neither through the use of language nor by any other means. If you're in pain, you can tell other people how much it hurts; however, you can't make them actually experience what you're going through. The same concept applies when we describe how we perceive colors. I'm the only person in the entire universe who knows what *my* blue looks like when I look at the sky. There is no way of certainly knowing that other people perceive colors in the same way as I do. Suffering is terrible, as anyone who went through a lot of pain or had close ones who did will know. I'm not trying to downplay the significant life-changing effects suffering can bring, but we need to keep in mind that, at the end of the day, it can and it ultimately does vary between individuals. Since conscious experiences differ in quality and intensity between each person, the only possible interpretation of the universe is a subjective one. Suffering is relative. Different people will experience painful events differently. We can't possibly know what it feels like to be someone else. If you've managed to go this far in life without going through times of severe distress, you're obviously very fortunate. Whether you ascribe your blessed circumstances to sheer luck or to a kind Creator, you're disqualified from having the "evil argument" in your debate arsenal about the nature of divinity. You simply don't and cannot possibly know what other conscious experiences than your own feel like.

How about if you feel that the suffering that you went through so far entitles you to question the existence of God or to doubt his benevolence? First of all, as we have seen at the beginning of the chapter, the notion of a well-intentioned divinity can be reconciled with mundane suffering. The key is replacing the human time scale for assessing one's condition with the cosmic one. The concept of a soul is deeply ingrained in the human mind and an afterlife could make the suffering experience in the limited time spent here on Earth utterly meaningless. There is simply too much we don't know. Perhaps God is more interested in humanity as a whole than in particular individuals? Maybe he's not omnipotent, as most religions have depicted him? Ultimately, what if he's not necessarily benevolent, even though the majority of people find their lives enjoyable enough to prevent them from committing suicide? Assuming that God must inevitably be good is Ivan Karamazov's fallacy. What if he is not, does it make this world look less like the product of an intelligent Designer? It is a question only you can answer.

Chapter 9

Conclusion

"Theory is good, but it doesn't prevent things from existing," the neurologist Jean-Martin Charcot once remarked. The 20th century began with the science of behaviorism telling everyone that thoughts, emotions, and feelings did not exist. As we saw earlier, behavioral psychology did not *need* people's inner lives, because they were not falsifiable. Consciousness was deemed unscientific and was dismissed as a result, but this didn't make it less real.

At the beginning of the 21st century, history seems to be repeating. We're told that God is not *needed* to explain the origin of the universe, the appearance of life, and the human mind's ability to link the physical world to the abstract realm of ideas. Despite the obvious gaps in modern theories, scientists vow to never again tolerate supernatural explanations in a rational view of the world. The notion of God must be banished at all costs, even if it means redefining science itself. As long as they fit the mainstream agenda, theories might even end up being considered true in the absence of experimental evidence to support their claims. The line between science and religion is becoming blurred, except this time, belief is discouraged. The middlemen between God and us have changed their purpose, but are still among us.

And yet, there will come a time when scientists looking back at our own period will find it difficult to believe that the idea of intelligent design was dismissed. Modern science is simply going through a denial of the divine phase. If it was able to refute direct experiences that everyone in the world had, is it unreasonable to worry that it is repeating the same mistake? We saw how *feelings* helped provide a better understanding of the human mind. Maybe they can do the same for the origin of life and the universe. There is a wide-spread *feeling* that something is amiss with the current theories meant to explain the fundamental truths about our world. The notion of God is deeply ingrained in our minds, and it is backed by abundant physical evidence, which only grows as we uncover new layers of complexity. Instead of dismissing it as a foolish emotional trap, could we perhaps use it to enhance our understanding of the universe?

Some might wonder if such an approach is even relevant. Since most people are religious anyway, despite the scientific consensus, why bother? It would seem that science and religion are bound to maintain their non-overlapping positions for a long time to come, and both sides are immune to persuasion efforts. This might very well be true, but there are always those caught in the middle, who identify religions as figments of the imagination and, despite believing in the power of reason, can also see that the current scientific explanations just don't add up. They form the target audience for my book, and if you're one of them, I hope I was at least able to put some doubt in your mind regarding the scientific "facts" you're constantly exposed to. Thinking for yourself remains your best option.

Notes

1 Cited in Michael J. Behe (1996) *Darwin's Black Box*, Free Press, New York, p. 9.

2 Behe, p. 193.

3 Paley, W. (2008) *Natural Theology*, Oxford University Press, New York, pp. 7-8.

4 Behe, p. 173.

5 Orr, H. A. (1996) "Darwin v. Intelligent Design (Again)" *Boston Review*, Dec/Jan. Retrieved March 3, 2021, from https://joelvelasco.net/teaching/2300/orr_review_behe.pdf

6 Dunham, W. (2017) "Canadian bacteria-like fossils called oldest evidence of life". Retrieved March 3, 2021, from https://www.reuters.com/article/topNews/idCAKBN16858B?edition-redirect=ca

7 Nagel, T. (2012) *Mind and Cosmos*, Oxford University Press, New York, p. 5.

8 Seneca (2004) *On the Shortness of Life*, Penguin Books, London, pp. 41-42.

9 Hawking S. (2016) *A Brief History of Time,* Transworld Publishers, London, pp. 49-50.

10 Koren, M. (2017) "Are We Living in a Giant Cosmic Void?". Retrieved March 3, 2021, from https://www.theatlantic.com/science/archive/2017/06/home-sweet-void/529623/

11 Krauss, L. M. (2012) *A Universe from Nothing*, Simon & Schuster, London, p. 4.

12 Berlinski, D. (2009) *The Devil's Delusion*, Basic Books, New York, p 87.

13 Cited in Behe, p. 244.

14 Knapton, S. (2020) "An earlier universe existed before the Big Bang, and can still be observed today, says Nobel winner". Retrieved March 4, 2021, from https://www.telegraph.co.uk/news/2020/10/06/earlier-universe-existed-big-bang-can-observed-today/

15 Krauss, p. 153.

[16] Gould, S. J. (1991) *Bully for Brontosaurus*, W. W. Norton & Company, New York, pp. 429-430.

[17] Susskind, L. (2006) *The Cosmic Landscape*, Back Bay Books, New York, p. 78.

[18] Krauss, p. 125.

[19] Linde, A. (2017) "A brief history of the multiverse", arXiv:1512.01203v3

[20] Hossenfelder, S. (2017) "What Quantum Gravity Needs Is More Experiments". Retrieved March 4, 2021, from https://nautil.us/issue/45/power/what-quantum-gravity-needs-is-more-experiments

[21] Wigner, E. (1960) "The Unreasonable Effectiveness of Mathematics in the Natural Sciences". Retrieved March 4, 2021, from https://www.maths.ed.ac.uk/~v1ranick/papers/wigner.pdf

[22] Susskind, p. 196.

[23] Susskind, p. 177.

[24] Axe, D. (2016) *Undeniable,* HarperOne, New York, p. 38.

[25] Dawkins, R. (2006) *The God Delusion*, Black Swan, London, p. 13.

[26] Dawkins, p. 173.

[27] Susskind, p. 355.

[28] Pinker, S. (1998) *How the Mind Works*, Allen Lane, London, p. 555.

[29] Dawkins, p. 205.

[30] Bloom, P. (2007) "Religion is natural". Retrieved March 4, 2021, from https://minddevlab.yale.edu/sites/default/files/files/Religion%20is%20natural.pdf

[31] Nagel, T. (1974) "What Is It Like to Be a Bat?". Retrieved March 4, 2021, from https://warwick.ac.uk/fac/cross_fac/iatl/study/ugmodules/humananimalstudies/lectures/32/nagel_bat.pdf

[32] Solms, M. (2021) *The Hidden Spring*, Profile Books, London, p. 107.

[33] Solms, p. 3.

[34] Hoffman, D. D. (2020) *The Case Against Reality*, Penguin Books, p. 14.

[35] Flew, A. (2007) *There is a God*, HarperOne, New York, pp. 88-89.

[36] Leibniz, G. W. (1991) *Discourse on Metaphysics*, Hackett Publishing, Indianapolis, p. 22.

[37] Leibniz, p. 24.

[38] Dawkins, p. 16.

[39] Hoffman, pp. 200-201.

Notes

40 Dostoevsky, F. (2009) *The Karamazov Brothers*, Wordsworth Classics, Ware, pp. 264-268.

41 Cited in Behe, p. 234.

Index

About the Author

Christian Bandea has a Master's degree in contemporary literature. After working for seven years as a journalist, he has built a successful IT career as a network engineer and developer. He lives near Cambridge, UK, with his wife and daughter.

Printed in Great Britain
by Amazon

35818328R00067